The Miracles of
Smith Wigglesworth

Dr Michael H Yeager

ISBN: 1506188036
ISBN-13: 9781506188034

DEDICATION

This is written for those who truly hunger and thirst after all that God has made available through the life, ministry, sufferings, death and resurrection of Jesus Christ . My prayer is that not only will your life be touched by these **divine miraculous occurrences**, but you yourself will truly step in to that realm where all things are possible .God is not a respecter of people, what he did for Smith Wigglesworth, he desires to do for you and me. May you experience wonderful transformation and divine healing.

These true stories have been modernized in order to make them more understandable and descriptive in our modern vernacular. All of the stories have been compiled from many different articles, books, stories, sermons, and writings of Smith Wigglesworth. There are acknowledgments at the beginning of each chapter to give credit to those who recorded the stories, and wrote them down for the increase and benefit of our personal faith. Jesus Christ is the same yesterday today and forever. What he did for these people he will do for you and me!

In this particular book about the Miracles Of Smith Wigglesworth you will discover 3 additional benefits !

#1 After every story you will discover a famous quote of Smith Wigglesworth. From the book: The Essential Smith Wigglesworth from Warner and Lee. Published in 1999

#2 In each chapter you will discover some wonderful spiritual insight of his teachings.

#3 At the end of each chapter you will be able to read a personal supernatural experiences that the writer of this book himself and his family have experienced .

CONTENTS

EXHORTATION

Smith Wigglesworth: This Is The Place Where God Will Show up!

You must come to a place of ashes, a place of helplessness, a place of wholehearted surrender where you do not refer to yourself. You have no justification of your own in regard to anything. You are prepared to be slandered, to be despised by everybody. But because of His personality in you, He reserves you for Himself because you are godly, and He sets you on high because you have known His name (Ps. 91:14). He causes you to be the fruit of His loins and to bring forth His glory so that you will no longer rest in yourself. Your confidence will be in God. Ah, it is lovely. "The Lord is the Spirit; and where the Spirit of the Lord is, there is liberty" (2 Cor. 3:17).

Born June 10th, 1859
Died March 4th, 1947

Dr Michael H Yeager

CHAPTER ONE

Romans 15:19
*Through **mighty signs** and wonders, by the power of the Spirit of God; so that from Jerusalem, and round about unto Illyricum, I have fully preached the gospel of Christ.*

***Galatians 3:5** He therefore that ministereth to you the Spirit, and worketh miracles among you, doeth he it by the works of the law, or by the hearing of faith?*

***Acts 4:33** And with great power gave the apostles witness of the resurrection of the Lord Jesus: and great grace was upon them all.*

***Acts 6:8** And Stephen, full of faith and power, did great wonders and miracles among the people.*

__1 Corinthians 2:4__ And my speech and my preaching was not with enticing words of man's wisdom, but in demonstration of the Spirit and of power:⁵ That your faith should not stand in the wisdom of men, but in the power of God.

From the book: Smith Wigglesworth a man who walked with God by George Stormont

#1   I had great compassion for the sick and needy before God ever started using me. One day a group of spiritual leaders came and said to me: "Smith We want to go to the Keswick convention, we have been thinking whom we should leave to do the work. We can only think of you." I said, "I couldn't conduct a healing service." They said, "We have no one else. We trust you to take care of the work while we are away." A thought came into my mind: "Well, any number of people can talk. All I have to do is to take charge." The following week when I got there the place was full of people. Of course, the first thing I did was to look for someone who would do the speaking; but everyone I asked said, "No, you have been chosen and you must do it." And so I had to begin. I do not remember what I said that night but I do know that when I had finished speaking fifteen people came forward for healing. One of these was a man from Scotland who was hobbled on a pair of crutches. I prayed for him and he was instantly healed. There was no one more surprised than I was. He was jumping all over the place without his crutches. This encouraged the others who were there to believe God for their healing and all of these people were healed. I am sure it was not my faith, but it was God in His compassion coming to help me in that hour of need.

Smith - "If I read the newspaper I come out dirtier than I went in. If I read my Bible, I come out cleaner than I went in, and I like being clean!"

#2 The Lord opened the door of faith for me more and more. I announced that I would have a Divine Healing meeting in Bradford on a certain evening. I can remember that there were twelve people who came that night and all of those twelve were miraculously healed. One had a tongue badly bitten in the center through a fall. This one was perfectly healed. Another was a woman with an ulcer on her ankle joint and a large sore that was constantly discharging. She was healed and there was only a scar the next day. The others were healed the same way.

Smith- "Some people like to read their Bibles in the Hebrew; some like to read it in the Greek; I like to always ready it in the Holy Spirit."

#3 One morning our children were all gathered around the breakfast table and my wife said, "Harold and Ernest are very sick this morning. Before we have breakfast we will go pray for them." Immediately the power of God fell upon my wife and me, and as we laid our hands on our children they were both instantly healed. As we saw the miraculous healing wrought before our eyes, we were both filled with intense joy. The Lord was always so good in proving Himself our family Physician.

Smith - "If you are in the same place today as you were yesterday, you are a backslider."

#4 One day a man asked me, "Does Divine Healing embrace seasickness? "I answered, "Yes. It is a spirit of fear that causes your seasickness, and I command that spirit to go out of you in Jesus' name." He was never seasick again from that day forward, though he had to travel much.

Smith - "In me is working a power stronger than every other power. The life that is in me is a thousand times bigger than I am outside."

#5 One day a man came to our house. He was a very devoted brother. I said to him, "Mr. Clark, you seem downcast today. What's up?" He answered, "I left my wife dying. Two doctors have been with her right through the night and they say she cannot live long." I said to him, "Why don't you believe God for your wife?" He answered, "Brother Wigglesworth, I cannot believe for her."

He went out of the house broken-hearted. Immediately I went to see a brother named Howe who was opening a small mission in Bradford. I thought he was the right man to go with me, in order to assist me. When I said, "Will you go with me?" he answered, "No, indeed I won't. Please do not ask me again. But I believe if you will go, God will heal." I realized then that the Lord put those words in his mouth to encourage me.

Well, I knew a man another brother named Nichols who, if he got the opportunity to pray, would pray all around the world three times and then come back. So I went to him and said, "Will you come with me to pray for Sister Clark?"

He answered, "Yes, I will be very glad." We had a mile and a half to walk to that house. I told him when he began to pray not to stop until he was finished. When we got to the house we saw that Mrs. Clark was almost dead. I said to the one I had brought with me, "You see the dangerous condition of Sister Clark. Now don't waste time but begin to pray." Seeing he had an opportunity, he began.

I had never heard or suffered so much unbelief or unnecessary prayer as I did when he was praying, and I cried to the Lord, "Stop him! Please, Lord, stop this man's praying." Why? Because he prayed for the dear husband who was going to be bereaved and for the children who were going to be motherless. He piled it on so thick that I had to cry out, "Stop him, Lord; I cannot stand this." And thank God, he stopped.

Though I knew that neither Clark nor Nichols believed in Divine Healing, I had concealed a small bottle in my hip pocket that would hold about half a pint of oil. I put a long cork in it so that I could open the bottle easily. I took the bottle out of my pocket and held it behind me, and said: "Now you pray, Mr. Clark." Brother Clark, being encouraged by Brother Nichols' prayer, prayed also that he might be sustained in his great bereavement. I could not stand it at all, and I cried, "Lord, stop him." I was so earnest and so broken that they could hear me outside the house. Thank God, he stopped.

As soon as he stopped, I pulled the cork out of the bottle, and went over to the dying woman who was laid out on the bed. I was very young in the faith when it came to Divine healing at this time and did not know any better, so I poured all of the contents of that bottle of oil over Mrs. Clark's body in the name of Jesus!

I was standing beside her at the top of the bed and looking towards the foot, when suddenly the Lord Jesus Himself appeared to me. I had my eyes open looking right at Him. There He was at the foot of the bed. He gave me one of those gentle smiles. I see Him just now as I tell this story to you. I have never lost that vision, the vision of that beautiful soft smile upon the face of Jesus. After a few moments He vanished but something happened that day that changed my whole life forever. Mrs. Clark was raised up and filled with life. She lived to bring up a number of children; she even outlived her husband by many years.

Smith - "It is better to live ready than to get ready!"

#6 My wife and I were both very zealous for the Lord and spent a great deal of time in open-air meetings. One Sunday a violent pain gripped me so deep it brought me down to the ground. Two men supported me and brought me home. The same thing had happened before but the pain had not been near as severe in previous times. My wife and I prayed all night. The next morning I said to my wife, "It seems to me that this is my home-call. We have been praying all night, and nothing has happened; I am worse. It does not seem as though anything can be done. You know our agreement is that when we know we have received a home-call, (dyeing) only then to save each other the embarrassment of having an inquest and the condemnation of outsiders, would we call a Doctor. I said to her: to protect yourself you should now call a physician. But I leave it with you to do what you think should be done."

My poor wife was in a sad plight, with all the little children around her and there seemed to be no hope whatever. She began to weep and left me to go and get a physician—not for him to help me, because she did not think he could help me in the least, but believing that the end of my life had come.

When the doctor came he examined me, shook his head, and said, "There is no hope whatever. He has had appendicitis for the past six months and the organs are in such shape that he is beyond hope." He turned to my wife and said, "I have to make a number of calls, Mrs. Wigglesworth. I will come and see you again later. The only hope is for him to have an immediate operation, but I am afraid your husband is too weak for that."

When he left the room, an elderly lady and a young man came to our house. She was a great woman of pray, and she believed that everything that was not of good health was of the Devil.

While she prayed, the young man laid his hands on me and cried out, **"Come out, Devil, in the name of Jesus."**

To my utter surprise I felt at that moment as well as I had ever felt in my life. I was absolutely free from pain. As soon as they had prayed for me they went downstairs, and I got up, believing that no one had a right to remain in bed when healed.

When I got downstairs, my wife cried, "Oh!" I said, "I am healed." She said, "I hope it is true." I inquired, "Any work to be done?" "Yes, there is a woman who is in a great hurry to get some plumbing done; if we could not take care of it, she would have to go somewhere else." She gave me the address and I went out to do this work.

While I was at work, the doctor returned. He put his silk hat on the table, went upstairs, and got as far as the landing, when my wife shouted, "Doctor! Doctor! Doctor!" He asked, "Are you calling me?" "Oh, Doctor, he's not here. He has gone out to work." The doctor answered, "They will bring him back a corpse, as sure as you live.

" Well, the "corpse" has been coming and going around the world preaching the Gospel these many years since that time! I have, laid hands on people with appendicitis in almost every part of the world and never knew of a case not instantly healed, even when doctors were on the premises.

Smith - "God has privileged us in Christ Jesus to live above the ordinary human plane of life. Those who want to be ordinary and live on a lower plane can do so, but as for me, I will not."

#7 One day Wigglesworth was at a farm being shown around by the owner, who was a dear friend. Visiting one field, he commented on the beauty of this man's property. But his friend said, "Brother Smith it is not what it looks like. The whole field is completely ruined by blight."

At that moment Wigglesworth lifted his heart to God. Faith flowed from his heart, and he stretched out his hand over the field speaking the name of Jesus. The field was completely cleansed of blight and the entire crop was saved. In fact, that was the best crop his friend said he had ever had from any previous years!

Smith - "The Spirit reveals, unfolds, takes of the things of Christ and shows them to us, and prepares us to be more than a match for satanic forces."

From the Book: EVER INCREASING FAITH by Smith Wigglesworth

 # 8 In Oakland, Calif., we were having a meeting in a very large theatre. So many came to that place that in order to accommodate everyone we had to have overflow meetings. There was a rising tide of people getting saved in the meeting by rising voluntarily up and down in the place, and getting saved. And then we had a large group of people who needed help in their bodies, rising in faith and being healed. One of these people was an old man 95 years of age. He had been suffering for three years, till he got to the place where for three weeks he had been taking liquids. He was in a terrible state. I got him to stand while I prayed for him; and he came back, and with a shining face, told us that new life had come into his body.

Later when he testified he had this testimony: He said, "I am 95 years old. When I came into the meeting, I was full of pain from cancer of the stomach. But now I have been so healed that I have been eating perfectly, and have no pain." Many of the people were healed in a similar way.

Smith - "How great is the position of the man who is born of God, born of purity, born of faith, born of life, born of power!"

Excerpt from the book: "Faith That Prevails"

#9   In one particular meeting a lady arose who had a bad case of rheumatism in the left leg. After being prayed for, she ran the full length of the hall several times, then testified to partial healing. A young man with pain in the head was healed instantly. Another man with pain in the shoulder was healed instantly also.

Smith - "If you want to increase in the life of God, then you must settle it in your heart that you will not at any time resist the Holy Spirit. The Holy Ghost and fire - the fire burning up everything that would hurt and destroy your walk with God."

#10   I will never forget the face of a man that came to me one time. His clothes hung from him, his whole frame was shrivelled, and his eyes were glaring and glassy, his jawbones stuck out, his whole being was a manifestation of death. He said to me, "Can you help me?" Could I help him?

I told him if we believe the **Word of God** can we help anybody, but we must be sure we are basing our faith on the Word of God. If we are on the Word of God then what God has promised will happen. I looked at him and I told him that I had never seen anybody that was still alive that looked like him. I said, "What is wrong with you? He answered with a small whisper of a voice, "I had a cancer in my chest. I was operated on and in removing this cancer they also removed my swallower; so now I can breathe but I cannot swallow."

He pulled out a tube about nine inches long with a cup at the top and an opening at the bottom to go into a hole. He showed me that he pressed one part of that into his stomach and poured liquid into the top; it was like he was a walking dead man. I said to him:" *... whosoever ... shall not doubt in his heart, but shall believe that those things which he saith shall come to pass; he shall have saith" (Mark 11:23).*
Based upon this reality I said to him "You shall have a good supper tonight." But, he said "I cannot swallow." I said, "You shall have a good supper tonight." But he repeated "I cannot swallow." ..... I said, "You shall have a good supper; now go and eat."

When he got home he told his wife that the preacher said he could eat a good supper that night. He said, "If you will get something ready I'll see if I can swallow." His wife prepaired a good supper and he took a mouthful. When he had tried to eat before the food would not go down. But the Word of God said "whatsoever," and this mouthful went down, and more and more went down until he was completely filled up! Then what happened? He went to bed with the joy of the knowledge that he could again swallow, and he awoke the next morning with the same joy! He looked for the hole in his stomach, but God had shut that hole in his stomach up.

Smith - "The secret of spiritual success is a hunger that persists...It is an awful condition to be satisfied with one's spiritual attainments... God was and is looking for hungry, thirsty desperate people."

#11   I was taken to see a beautiful nine-year-old boy who was lying on a bed. The mother and father were extremely distraught because he had been lying there in bed for months. They had to lift and feed him; he was like a cold statue with flashing eyes. As soon as I entered the place the Lord revealed to me the cause of the trouble with a word of knowledge, so I said to the mother, "The Lord shows me there is something wrong with his stomach." She said, "Oh no, we have had two physicians and they say it is paralysis of the mind." I said, "God reveals to me it is his stomach." "Oh, no, it isn't. These physicians ought to know, they have x-rayed him."

The gentleman who brought me there said to the mother, "You have sent for this man, it is because of you that he has come, now please allow him to help. I prayed over this boy and laid my hands on his stomach. After I prayed He became sick and vomited up a worm thirteen inches long and was perfectly and completely restored.

Smith - "Never listen to human plans. God can work mightily when you persist in believing Him in spite of discouragement from the human standpoint. ... I am moved by what I believe. I know this: no man looks at the circumstances if he believes."

#12   I know of a situation where six people went into the house of a sick man to pray for him. He was an Episcopalian priest, and he laid in his bed utterly helpless, without even strength to help himself. He had read a little tract about Divine healing and had heard about people praying for the sick, and sent for some of my friends, who, he thought, could pray the prayer of faith. He was anointed according to *James 5:14*, but, he had no immediate manifestation of healing, he wept bitterly. The six people walked out of the room, somewhat discouraged to see the man lying there in an unchanged condition.

When they were outside, one of the six said, "There is one thing we should have done. I wish you would all go back with me and let's try it." They all went back and got together in a group. This brother said, "Let us whisper the name of **Jesus**." At first when they whispered this wonderful worthy name nothing seemed to happen. But as they continued to whisper, **"Jesus! Jesus! Jesus!** In Faith , sincerity and Love" the power of God began to fall. As they saw that God was beginning to work, their faith and joy increased; and they whispered the name of **Jesus Christ** louder and louder. As they did so the man suddenly arose from his bed and dressed himself. The secret was simply this, those six people had got their eyes off the sick man, and put their eyes upon the **Lord Jesus** Himself, their faith grasped the power and authority that there is in the name that's above every name of **Jesus Christ** of Nazareth.

Smith - "Enter into the promises of God. It is your inheritance. You will do more in one year if you are really filled with the Holy Ghost than you could do in fifty years apart from Him."

From the book: "Ever Increasing Faith" Sermon Titled: Gifts and Healings

#13 I was called at 10 o'clock one night to pray for a young lady given up by the doctor. She was dying of consumption. As I looked, I saw that unless God did something it was impossible for her to live. I turned to the mother and said, "Well, mother, you will have to go to bed." She said, "Oh, I have not changed my clothes for three weeks." I said to the daughters, "You will also have to go to bed," but they did not want to go. It was the same with the son.

I put on my overcoat and said, well if you will not cooperate "Good-bye, I'm leaving." They said, "Oh, don't leave us." I said, "I can do nothing here if you do not go to bed." They said, "Oh, if you will stop, we will all go to bed." I knew that God could not move in the least in an atmosphere of just natural sympathy and unbelief.

They all went to bed and I stayed, and that was surely a battle as I knelt by that bed face to face with death and with the devil. But God can change the hardest situation and make you know that He is almighty.

Then the real fight came. It seemed as though the heavens were brass. I prayed from 11 to 3:30 in the morning. As I was praying I saw the light in this young ladies face leave and she died. The devil said, "Now you are done for. You have come from Bradford and this girl has died on your hands." I said, "It can't be. God did not send me here for nothing. Now this is the time to take a hold of violent Faith." I remembered that passage which said, "Men ought always to pray and not to faint." Death had taken place but I knew that my God was all-powerful, and He that had split the Red Sea is just the same today. It was a time when I would not and could not have "No," for an answer, but in the mist of the fight of faith God said "**Yes**." I looked at the window and at that moment the face of **Jesus** appeared to me. It seemed as though a million rays of light were coming from His face. As He looked at the one who had just passed away, the colour came back to her face. At that moment she rolled over and fell asleep. Oh my then I had a glorious time. In the morning she woke early, put on a dressing gown and walked to the piano. She started to play and to sing a wonderful song. The mother and the sister and the brother had all come down to listen. The Lord had undertaken. A miracle had been wrought.

Smith - "Fear looks; faith jumps. Faith never fails to obtain its object. If I leave you as I found you, I am not God's channel. I am not here to entertain you, but for you to be at place where you can laugh at the impossible."

TEACHING FROM SMITH WIGGLESWOTH

*WHY PEOPLE ARE SICK

Where people are in sickness you find frequently that they are dense about Scripture. They usually know three scriptures though. They know about Paul's thorn in the flesh, and that Paul told Timothy to take a little wine for his stomach's sake, and that Paul left someone sick somewhere; they forget his name, and don't remember the name of the place, and don't know where the chapter is. Most people think they have a thorn in the flesh. The chief thing in dealing with a person who is sick is to locate their exact position. As you are ministering under the Spirit's power the Lord will let you see just that which will be more helpful and most faith-inspiring to them.

*WHY MANY BELIEVERS ARE NOT HEALED!

I realize that God can never bless us on the lines of being hardhearted, critical or unforgiving. This will hinder faith quicker than anything. I remember being at a meeting where there were some people tarrying for the Baptism-seeking for cleansing, for the moment a person is cleansed the Spirit will fall. There was one man with eyes red from weeping bitterly. He said to me, "I shall have to leave. It is no good my staying without I change things. I have written a letter to my brother-in-law, and filled it with hard words, and this thing must first be straightened out." He went home and told his wife, "I'm going to write a letter to your brother and ask him to forgive me for writing to him the way I did." "You fool!" she said. "Never mind," he replied, "this is between God and me, and it has got to be cleared away." He wrote the letter and came again, and straightway God filled him with the Spirit.

I believe there are a great many people who would be healed, but they are harboring things in their hearts that are as a blight. Let these things go. Forgive, and the Lord will forgive you. There are many good people, people that mean well, but they have no power to do anything

24

for God. There is just some little thing that came in their hearts years ago, and their faith has been paralyzed ever since. Bring everything to the light. God will sweep it all away if you will let Him. Let the precious blood of Christ cleanse from all sin. If you will but believe, God will meet you and bring into your lives the sunshine of His love.

EXPERIENCES FROM THE AUTHOR

My Supernatural Salvation

It was my nineteenth birthday (February 18, 1975). I was in the Navy at the time and heavily involved in alcohol, drugs, and other ungodly activities. I had decided to commit suicide. I do not remember anyone ever sharing the gospel of Jesus Christ with me. No one ever took the time to warn me about eternal damnation for those who did not know God. I was overwhelmed with self-pity and depression. I went into the bathroom with a large, survival hunting knife. I put the knife to my wrist with full intentions of slitting my artery. I was determined to kill myself. I held the knife firmly against my wrist and took one more last breath before I slid it across my wrist. All of a sudden, invisible presence came rushing down upon me like a blanket. It was a tangible, overwhelming presence of mind-boggling fear. It was the fear of God, and it overwhelmed me! Instantly, I realized with crystal-clear understanding that I was going to hell. I deserved hell; I belonged in hell, and hell had a right to me. Furthermore, I knew if I slit my wrist, I would be in hell forever.

Overwhelming Love

I walked out of that little military bathroom to my bunk. I fell on my knees, reached my hands up toward heaven and cried out to Jesus with all of my heart. All of this was supernatural and strange. I did not ever recall any time when anyone ever shared with me how to become a Christian or how to be converted. Yet, I knew how to pray. I cried out to Jesus and told Him I believed He was the Son of God, had been raised from the dead, and I desperately needed Him. I not only asked Him into my heart but I gave Him my heart, soul, mind, and life. At that very instant, a love beyond description came rushing into my heart. I really knew what love was for the first time in my life. At the same time, I comprehended what I was placed on this earth for—I was here to follow, love, serve, and obey God. A deep love and hunger to know God grabbed my heart. I was filled with love from top to bottom, inside and out— inexpressibly beyond belief. Jesus had come to live inside of me!

Instantaneous Deliverance

I was instantly delivered: from over three packs of cigarettes a day, from worldly and satanic music, from chewing tobacco; from cussing and swearing, from drugs and alcohol, and from a filthy and dirty mind.

Some might ask why my conversion was so dramatic. I believe that it's because I had nothing to lose. I knew down deep that there was not one single thing worth saving in me. The only natural talent I ever possessed was the ability to mess things up. At the moment of salvation, I completely surrendered my heart and life to Jesus Christ.

My Tongue Was Loosed

Hunger and thirst for the Word of God began to possess me. I devoured Matthew, Mark, Luke, and John. Jesus became my hero in every area of my thoughts and daily life. He became my reason for getting up and going to work, eating, sleeping, and living. I discovered that everything I did was based on the desire of wanting to please Him.

One day I was reading my Bible and discovered where Jesus said that when He left the earth He would send to us the Holy Ghost to make us a witness. Furthermore, I learned it was His will for me to be filled with the Holy Ghost and that the Holy Ghost would make me a witness to others as He led and guided me into all truth.

I desperately wanted to reach the lost for Jesus Christ so they could experience the same love and freedom that I had experienced. I remember getting on my knees next to my bunk where I cried out and asked God to fill me with the Holy Ghost so I could be a witness. At that very moment, it felt like hot buckets of oil was being poured upon me. Something began to rise up out of my innermost being. Before I knew what happened, a new language came out of my mouth. I began to speak in a heavenly tongue.

Prior to this time I had a terrible speech impediment and could not even pronounce my own last name properly. After I prayed in this new language, I discovered my speech impediment was instantly and completely gone! From that time on, I have never stopped talking. Every chance I have, I share the truth of Jesus Christ with others.

CHAPTER TWO

From Sermon : God-Given Faith

#14   I remember being one day in Lancashire, and going round to see some sick people. I was taken into a house where there was a young woman lying on a bed, a very helpless case. The reason had gone, and many things were manifested there which were satanic and I knew it. She was only a young woman, a beautiful child. The husband, quite a young man, came in with the baby, and he leaned over to kiss the wife. The moment he did, she threw herself over on the other side, just as a lunatic would do. That was very heart-breaking. Then he took the baby and pressed the baby's lips to the mother. Again another wild kind of thing happened. I asked one who was attending her, "Have you sought anybody to help?" "Oh," they said, "We have had many professionals." "But," I said, "have you no spiritual help?" Her husband stormed out, saying, "Help? You think that we believe in God, after we have had seven weeks of no sleep and these maniac conditions."

Then a young woman of about eighteen or so just grinned at me and passed out of the door. That brought me to a place of compassion for the woman. Something had to be done, no matter what it was. Then with all my faith I began to penetrate the heavens, and I was soon out of that house, I will tell you, for I never saw a man get anything from God who prayed on the earth. If you get anything from God, you will have to reach into heaven; for it is all there. If you are living in the earth realm and expect things from heaven, they will never come. And as I saw, in the presence of God, the limitations of my faith, there came another faith, a faith that could not be denied, a faith that took the promise, a faith that believed God's Word. And from that presence, I came back again to earth, but not the same man. God gave me a faith that could shake hell and anything else.

I said, "**Come out of her, in the name of Jesus!**" And she rolled over and fell asleep and awoke in fourteen hours perfectly sane and perfectly whole.

Smith - "How can one come to possess great faith? Now listen, here is the answer to that: First, the blade, then the ear, then the full corn in the ear. Faith must grow by soil, moisture, and exercise."

Sermon: Like Precious Faith

#15   When I was going over to New Zealand and Australia, I had many to see me off. There was an Indian doctor who was riding in the same car with me to the docks. He was very quiet and took in all things that were said on the ship. I began to preach, of course, and the Lord began to work among the people. In the second-class part of the ship there was a young man and his wife who were attendants on a lady and gentleman in the first-class. And as these two young people heard me talking to them privately and otherwise, they were very much impressed. Then the lady they were attending got very sick. In her sickness and her loneliness she could find no relief. They called in the doctor, and the doctor gave her no hope.

And then, when in this strange dilemma –(she was a great Christian Scientist, a preacher of it, and had gone up and down preaching it)-- they thought of me. Knowing the conditions, and what she lived for, that it was late in the day, and that in the condition of her mind she could only receive the simplest words, I said to her, "Now you are very sick, and I won't talk to you about anything save this; I will pray for you in the name of Jesus, and the moment I pray you will be healed."

And the moment I prayed she was healed. That was this like precious faith in operation. Then she was disturbed. Now I could have poured in oil very soon. But I poured in all the bitter truth possible, and for three days I had her on nothing cinders and conviction. I showed her true terrible state, and pointed out to her all her folly and the fallacy of her position. I showed her that there was nothing in Christian Science, that it is a pure lie from the beginning, one of the major deceptions of hell. At best a lie, preaching a lie, and producing a lie.

Then she woke up to her true condition. She became extremely penitent and broken-hearted. But the thing that touched her first was that she had to go to preach the simple gospel of Christ where she had preached Christian Science. She asked me if she had to give up certain things. I won't mention the things, they are too vile. I said, "What you have to do is to see Jesus and take Jesus." When she saw the Lord in His purity, the other things had to go. At the presence of the real Jesus all else goes.

This opened the door to the rest of those on the boat. I had a wonderful opportunity to preach to all of the passengers. As I preached, the power of God fell, conviction came and sinners were saved. People began to follow me into my cabin one after another. God was working in a wonderful way.

In the mist of all of this activity a Indian doctor came. He said, "What shall I do? I cannot use medicine anymore." "Why?" "Oh, your preaching has changed me. But I must have a foundation. Will you spend some time with me?" "Of course I will." Then we

31

went alone and God broke the hardened ground of his heart. This Indian doctor decided that he was going right back to his nation with a new purpose. He had left a practice there. He told me of the great influence he had on many people. He was determined to go back to his practice to preach Jesus Christ.

Smith - "The Bible is the Word of God: supernatural in origin, eternal in duration, inexpressible in valor, infinite in scope, regenerative in power, infallible in authority, universal in interest, personal in application, inspired in totality. Read it through, write it down, pray it in, work it out, and then pass it on. Truly it is the Word of God. It brings into man the personality of God; it changes the man until he becomes the epistle of God. It transforms his mind, changes his character, takes him on from grace to grace, and gives him an inheritance in the Spirit. God comes in, dwells in, walks in, talks through, and sups with him."

Sermon: Spiritual Power

#16   A woman came to me in Cardiff, Wales, who was filled with an ulceration. She had fallen in the streets twice through this trouble. She came to the meeting and it seemed as if the evil power within her was trying to kill her right there, for she fell, and the power of the devil was extremely brutal. She was helpless, and it seemed as if she had died right there on the spot. I cried,

"O God, help this woman." Then I rebuked the evil power in the name of Jesus, and instantly right then and there the Lord healed her. She rose up and was so filled with excitement and joy that we could not keep her quiet. She felt the power of God in her body and wanted to testify all the time. After three days she went to another place and began to testify about the Lord's power to heal the sick and the demonically oppressed. She came to me and said, "I want to tell everyone about the Lord's healing power. Have you no tracts on this subject?" I handed her my Bible and said, "Matthew, Mark, Luke, John--they are the best tracts on healing. They are full of incidents about the power of Jesus. They will never fail to accomplish the work of God if people will believe them."

Smith - "There is nothing impossible with God. All the impossibility is with us when we measure God by the limitations of our unbelief."

#17   I had been preaching on this line in Toronto, endeavoring to show that the moment a man believes with all of his heart that God puts into him a reality, a substance, a life; yea, God dwells in him, and with the new birth there comes into us a mighty force that is mightier than all the power of the enemy. Well one of the men who was at this meeting ran right out after the service, and when I got home that night this man was there with a big, distinguishing, tall man. This distinguished -looking man said to me, "Three years ago my nerves became shattered. I can't sleep. I have lost my business. I have lost everything. I am not able to sleep at all and my life is one of misery." I said to him, "Go home and sleep in the name of Jesus." He turned around and seemed reluctant to go; but I said to him, "Go!" and shoved him out of the door.

The next morning he called up on the telephone. He said to my host, "Tell Smith Wigglesworth I slept all night. I want to see him at once." He came and said, "I'm a new man. I feel I have new life. And now can you get me my money back?" I said, "Everything!"

He said, "Tell me how." I said, "Come to the meeting tonight and I'll tell you." The power of God was mightily present in that evening meeting, and he was greatly under conviction. He made for the altar, but fell before he got there. The Lord changed him and everything in him and about him. He is now a successful businessman. All his past failures had come through a lack of the knowledge of God. No matter what troubles you, God can shake the devil out of you, and completely transform you. There is none like Him in all of creation.

Smith - "If it is in the Bible, it is so. It's not even to be prayed about. It's to be received and acted upon. Inactivity is a robber which steals blessings. Increase comes by action, by using what we have and know. Your life must be one of going on from faith to faith."

#18   One day I was traveling on a railway train where there were two sick people in the car, a mother and her daughter. I said to them, "Look, I've something in this bag that will cure every affliction in the world. It has never been known to fail." They became very much interested, and I went on telling them more about this remedy that has never failed to remove disease and sickness. At last they summoned up courage to ask for a dose. So I opened my bag, took out my Bible, and read them that verse, "I am the Lord that healeth thee." It never fails. He will heal you if you dare believe Him. Men are searching everywhere today for things with which they can heal themselves, and they ignore the fact that the Balm of Gilead is within easy reach. As I talked about this wonderful Physician, the faith of both mother and daughter reached out to Christ, and as I prayed for them Jesus healed them both, right in the train.

Smith - "You must be yielded to the Word of God. The Word will cause love to begin to flow in our hearts like a River, and when divine love is in our hearts, there is no room to boast about ourselves. We see ourselves as nothing when we get lost in this divine love."

#19   A man came to me one time, brought to me by a little woman. I said, "What's going on with him?" She said, "He gets into circumstances of being attempted, but he fails every time. He is a slave to alcohol and nicotine poison. He is a bright, intelligent man in most things, but he just gives in to those two things." I was reminded of the words of the Master, giving us power to bind and loose, and I told him to put out his tongue.

In the name of the Lord Jesus Christ I cast out the evil powers that gave him the taste for these things. I said to him, "Sir, you are free from today forward." He was unsaved, but when he realized the power of the Lord had delivered him, he came to the our meetings. He Publicly acknowledged that he was a sinner, and the Lord saved and baptized him right then and there. A few days later I asked, "How are things going with you?" He said, "I am delivered." God has given us the power to bind and the power to loose even the spirit of alcohol and nicotine. But in order to operate in this authority you must be submitted to that authority, the Lordship of Jesus Christ.

Smith - "You must come to see how wonderful you are in God and how helpless you are in yourself."

#20　　In another place a woman came to me and said, "I have not been able to smell for twenty years; can you do anything for me?" I said, "You will be able to smell tonight." Could I give anybody that which had been lost for twenty years? Not of myself, but I remembered the Rock on which God's church is built, the Rock Christ Jesus, and His promise to give to His own the power to bind and loose. We can dare to do anything if we know we have the Word of God hidden in our hearts, submitted to in every regards. In the name of the Lord Jesus I loosed this woman. She ran all the way home. The table was full of all kinds of good food, but she would not touch a thing. She said, "I am having a feast of just being able to smell again!" Praise the Lord for the fact that He Himself, Christ Jesus backs up his own Word and proves the truth of it in these days of unbelief and apostasy.

Smith - "Faith is just the open door through which the Lord comes. Do not say, 'I was saved by faith' or 'I was healed by faith.' Faith does not save and heal. God saves and heals through that open door. You believe, and the power of Christ comes."

#21　　Another person came and said, "What can you do for me? I have had sixteen operations and have had my ear drums taken out." I said, "God has not forgotten how to make ear drums." I anointed her and prayed in the name of Jesus Christ, asking the Lord that her ear drums should be replaced. She was so deaf that I do not think she would have heard had a cannon gone off. She seemed to be as deaf I prayed as she was before. But she saw other people getting healed and rejoicing. Has God forgotten to be gracious? Was His power just the same? She came the next night and said, "I have come tonight to believe God." Take care you do not come in any other way. I prayed for her again and commanded her ears to be loosed in the name of Jesus. She believed, and the moment she believed she heard, she ran and jumped upon a chair and began to preach right then and there. Later that night I let a pin drop next to her and she heard it fall. God can give new ear drums to your ears. All things are possible with God.

Smith - "Perfect love will never want the preeminence in everything, it will never want to take the place of another, it will always be willing to take the back seat."

Sermon: Paul's Pentecost

#22   As I was looking through my letters one day while in the city of Belfast, a man came up to me and said, "Are you visiting the sick?" He pointed me to go to a certain house and told me to go to it and there I would see a very sick woman. I went to the house and I saw a very helpless woman propped up in bed. I knew that humanly speaking she was beyond all help. She was breathing with short, sharp breaths as if every breath would be her last. I cried to the Lord and said, "Lord, tell me what to do." The Lord said to me, "Read the fifty-third chapter of Isaiah." I opened my Bible and did as I was told. I read down to the fifth verse of this chapter, when all of a sudden the woman shouted, **"I am healed! I am healed!"** I was amazed at this sudden exclamation and asked her to tell me what had happened. She said, "Two weeks ago I was cleaning house and I strained my heart very badly. Two physicians have been to see me, but they both told me there was no help. But last night the Lord gave me a vision. I saw you come right into my bedroom. I saw you praying. I saw you open your Bible at the fifty-third chapter of Isaiah. When you got down to the fifth verse and read the words, 'With His stripes we are healed,' I saw myself wonderfully healed. That was a vision, now it is a fact."

Smith - Seek God until you get from Him a mighty revelation of the Son that moves you to the place where you are always steadfast.

#23   There was a young man at the meeting this particular night who had been saved the night before. He was all on fire to get others saved and purposed in his heart that every day of his life he would get someone saved. He saw this dejected hangman and began to speak to him about his soul. He brought him down to our mission and there he came under a wonderful and mighty conviction of sin. For two and a half hours he was literally sweating under conviction and you could see a vapor rising up from him in the cold air. At the end of two and a half hours he was graciously saved.

I said, "Lord, tell me what to do now." The Lord said, "Don't leave him, but go home with him." I went to his house. When he saw his wife he said, "God has saved me." The wife broke down and she too was graciously saved. I tell you there was a difference in that home. Even the cat knew the difference.

There were two sons in that house and one of them said to his mother, "Mother, what is happening here in our home? It has never like then this before. It is so peaceful. What is it?" She told him, "Father has been gloriously saved." Both sons were gloriously saved.

I took this man with me to many special services and the power of God was on him for many days. He would give his testimony and as he grew in grace he desired to preach the gospel. He became a powerful evangelist and hundreds and hundreds were brought to a saving knowledge of the Lord Jesus Christ through his ministry. The grace of God is sufficient for the vilest. He can take the most wicked of men and make them monuments of his grace. He did this with Saul of Tarsus at the very time he was breathing out threatening's and slaughter against the disciples of the Lord. He did it with Berry the hangman. He will do it for hundreds more in response to our cries.

Smith - Never mind what it costs - it is worth everything to have His smile and His presence

#24   It was about thirty-one years ago that a man came to me and said, "Wigglesworth, do you know what is happening in Sunderland? People are being baptized in the Holy Ghost exactly the same way as the disciples were on the Day of Pentecost." I said, "I would like to go." I immediately took a train and went to Sunderland. I went to the meetings and said, "I want to hear these tongues." I was told, "When you receive the Baptism in the Holy Ghost, you will speak in tongues." I said, "I have the Baptism in the Holy Ghost." One man said, "Brother, when I received the Baptism I spoke in tongues." I said, "Let's hear you." But could not speak in tongues, he could only speak as the Spirit gave him utterance and so my curiosity was not satisfied.

I saw these people were very earnest and I became quite hungry. I was anxious to see this new manifestation of the Spirit and I would be questioning all the time and spoiling a lot of the meetings. One man said to me, "I am a missionary and I have come here to seek the Baptism in the Holy Ghost. I am waiting on the Lord, but you have come in and are spoiling everything with your questions." I began to argue with him and our love became so hot that when we walked home he walked on one side of the road and I on the other.

That night there was to be a waiting meeting and I purposed to go. I changed my clothes and left my key in the clothes I had taken off. As we came from the meeting in the middle of the night I found I did not have my key upon me and this missionary brother said, "You will have to come and sleep with me." But do you think we went to bed that night? Oh, no, we spent the night in prayer. We received a precious shower from above. The breakfast bell rang, but I was not hungry. For four days I wanted nothing but God. If you only knew the unspeakably wonderful blessings of being filled with the Third Person of the Trinity, you would set aside everything else to tarry for this infilling.

I was about to leave Sunderland. This revival was taking place in the vestry of an Episcopal Church. I went to the parsonage that day to say goodbye and I said to Sister Boddy, the vicar's wife, "I am going away, but I have not received the tongues yet." She said, "It isn't tongues you need, but the Baptism." I said, "I have the Baptism, Sister, but I would like to have you lay hands on me before I leave."

She laid her hands on me and then had to go out of the room. The fire fell. It was a wonderful time as I was there with God alone. It seemed as though God bathed me in power. I was given a wonderful vision. I was conscious of the cleansing of the precious blood and cried out, "Clean! Clean! Clean!" I was filled with the joy of the consciousness of the cleansing. I saw the Lord Jesus Christ. I saw the empty cross and I saw Him exalted at the right hand of God the Father. As I was extolling, magnifying, and praising Him I was speaking in tongues as the Spirit of God gave me utterance. I knew now that I had received the real Baptism in the Holy Ghost.

I sent a telegram home and when I got there one of our boys said, "Father, I hear you have been speaking in tongues. Let's hear you." I could not speak in tongues. I had been moved to speak in tongues as the Spirit of God gave utterance at the moment I received the Baptism, but I did not receive the gift of tongues and could not speak a word. I never spoke again in tongues until nine months later when I was praying for someone, and it was then that God gave me the permanent gift of speaking in tongues.

When I got home my wife said to me, "So you think you have received the Baptism of the Holy Ghost. Why, I am as much baptized in the Holy Ghost as you are." We had sat on the platform together for twenty years but that night she said, "Tonight you will be preaching to the congregation." I said, "All right." As I went up to the platform that night the Lord gave me the first few verses of the sixty-first chapter of Isaiah, "The Spirit of the Lord God is upon me; because the Lord hath anointed me to preach good tidings unto the meek: He hath sent me to bind up the broken-hearted, to proclaim liberty to the captives, and the opening of the prison to them that are bound."

My wife went back to one of the furthermost seats in the hall and she said to herself, "I will watch what happens." I preached that night on the subject the Lord had given me and I told what the Lord had done for me. I told the people that I was going to have God in my life and I would gladly suffer a thousand deaths rather than forfeit this wonderful infilling that had come to me. My wife was very restless. She was moved in a new way and said, "That is not my Smith that is preaching. Lord, you have done something for him." As soon as I had finished, the secretary of the mission got up and said, "Brethren, I want what the leader of our mission has got." He tried to sit down but missed his seat and fell on the floor. There were soon fourteen of them on the floor, my own wife included. We did not know what to do, but the Holy Ghost got hold of the situation and the fire fell. A revival started and the crowds came. It was only the beginning of the flood-tide of blessing. We had touched the reservoir of the Lord's life and power. Since that time the Lord has taken me to many different lands and I have witnessed many blessed outpourings of God's Holy Spirit.

Wigglesworth's reply to a woman who asked for books on healing. 'I handed her my Bible & said "Matthew, Mark, Luke & John' are the best"

Sermon: Keeping the Vision

#25   I was holding a meeting, once, in London, and at the close a man came to me and said, "We are now allowed to hold meetings in this hall after 11 o'clock, and we would like you to come home with us. I am so hungry for God." The wife said she, too, was hungry, and so I agreed to go with them. At about 12:30 we arrived at their house. The man began stirring up the cooking fire and said, "Now we will have a good supper." I said to them, "I did not come here for your warm fire, your supper or your bed. I came here because I thought you were hungry to get more of God." We got down to pray and at about 3:30 the Lord baptized the wife, and she spoke in tongues as the Spirit gave utterance. At about 5 o'clock I spoke to the husband and asked how he was getting on. He replied, "God has broken my iron, stubborn will." He had not received the Baptism, but God had wrought a mighty work within him.

The following day, at his business, everyone could tell that a great change had come to him. Before he had been a walking terror. The men who labored for him had looked upon him as a regular devil because of the way he had acted; but coming into contact with the power of God that night completely changed him.

Before this he had made a religious profession, but he had never truly entered into the experience of the new birth until that night, when the power of God surged so mightily through his home. A short while afterwards I went to this man's home, and his two sons ran to me and kissed me, saying, "We have a new father." Previous to this these boys had often said to their mother, "Mother, we cannot stand it in the home any longer. We will have to leave." But the Lord changed the whole situation that night as we prayed together. On the second visit the Lord baptized this man in the Holy Ghost. The Holy Spirit will reveal false positions, pull the mask off any refuge of lies and clean up and remove all false conditions. When the Holy Spirit came in, that man's house and business and he himself were entirely changed.

Smith - Read it through; write it down; pray it in; work it out; pass it on. The Word of God changes a person until they become an Epistle of God.

#26   I remember being in a meeting at one time, where there was a man seeking the Baptism, and he looked like he was in trouble. He was very restless, and finally he said to me, "I will have to go." I said, "What's up?" He said, "God is unveiling things to me, and I feel so unworthy." I said, "Repent of everything that is wrong." He continued to tarry and the Lord continued to search his heart. These times of waiting on God for the fullness of the Spirit are times when He searches the heart and tries the reins. Later the man said to me, "I have a hard thing to do, the hardest thing I have ever had to do." I said to him,

"Tell the Lord you will do it, and never mind the consequences." He agreed, and the next morning he had to take a ride of thirty miles and go with a bag of gold to a certain party with whom he dealt. This man owned a hundred cattle in which he had bought all of his feed for at a certain business. He always paid his accounts on a certain day, but one day he missed. He was always so punctual in paying his accounts that when later the people of this business went over their books, they thought they must have made a mistake in not crediting the man with the money and so they sent him a receipt that said it was paid. The man never intended not to pay the account, but if you delay to do a right thing the devil will see that you never do it. But when that man was seeking the Lord that night he was seeking for the baptism of the Holy Spirit the Lord dealt with him strongly on this point, and he had to go and correct the thing the next morning. He paid the account and then the Lord baptized him in the Spirit. They that bear the vessels of the Lord must be clean, must be holy.

Smith - "When the saint ceases to seek after holiness, purity, righteousness, truth; when he ceases to pray, stops reading the Word and gives way to carnal appetites, then it is that Satan comes."

#27   I was once traveling from Belgium to England. As I landed I received a request to stop at a place between Harwich and Colchester. The people were delighted that God had sent me, and told me of a special situation that they wanted me to pray for. They said, "We have a brother here who believes in the Lord, and he is paralyzed from his loins downward. He cannot stand on his legs and he has been twenty years in this condition." They took me to this man and as I saw him there in his chair I put the question to him. "What is the greatest desire in your heart?"

He said, "Oh, if I could only receive the Holy Ghost!" I was somewhat surprised at this answer, and I laid my hands on his head and said, "Receive ye the Holy Ghost." Instantly the power of God fell upon him and he began breathing very heavily. He rolled off the chair and there he lay like a bag of potatoes, utterly helpless. I love it when God is at moving. I like to watch God working. There he was with his great, fat body, and his head was swinging just as though it was on a swivel. Then to our joy he began speaking in a heavenly tongue. I had my eyes glued on him and as I saw the condition of his legs I said, "Those legs can never carry that body."

Then I looked up and said, "Lord, tell me what to do. "The Holy Ghost is the executive of Jesus Christ and the Father. If you want to know the mind of God you must have the Holy Ghost to bring God's latest thought to you and to tell you what to do. The Lord said to me, "Command him in My name to walk" But I missed it. I said to the people there, "Let's see if we can lift him up." But we could not lift him, he was like a ton weight. I cried, "Oh Lord, forgive me." I repented of doing the wrong thing, and then the Lord said to me again, "Command him to walk." I said to him, "Arise in the name of Jesus." His legs were immediately strengthened. Did he walk? YES! He ran all around. A month after this he walked ten miles and back. He has a Pentecostal work now. When the power of the Holy Ghost is present, things will happen.

Smith - "Great faith is the product of great fights. Great testimonies are the outcome of great tests. Great triumphs can only come out of great trials."

Sermon: Ye Shall Receive Power

#28   In Switzerland the people said to me, "How long can you preach for us?" I said to them, "When the Holy Ghost is upon me, we can preach forever!" When I was in San Francisco, driving down the main street one day, we came across a crowd in the street. The driver stopped and I jumped out of the car, and right across from where the tumult was, I found a boy lying on the ground apparently in the grip of death. I got down and asked, "What is wrong with you?" He replied in a whisper, "syphilis." I put my hand underneath his back and said, "In the name of Jesus, come out." At that moment the boy jumped up and ran away, not even stopping to say "Thank you."

Smith - As we think about that which is Holy, we become Holy. The more we think about Jesus, the more we become like Him.

#29   In Switzerland the people said to me, "How long can you preach to us?" I said to them, "When the Holy Ghost is upon us, we can preach forever!" When I was in San Francisco, driving down the main street one day, we came across a crowd in the street. The driver stopped and I jumped out of the car, and right across from where the tumult was, I found a boy lying on the ground apparently in the grip of death. I got down and asked, "What is amiss?" He replied in a whisper, "tramp." I put my hand underneath his back and said, "In the name of Jesus, come out." And the boy jumped up and ran away, not even stopping to say "Thank you."

Smith - Once on a train, the Spirit was so heavily upon me that my face shone. Within 3 minutes, everyone on the train was crying to God.

TEACHING FROM SMITH WIGGLESWOTH

* God Passes Over the Proud and Haughty!

God cannot trust some with the gift, but those who have a lowly, broken, contrite heart He can trust. One day I was in a meeting where there were a lot of doctors and eminent men, and many ministers. It was at a convention, and the power of God fell on the meeting. One humble little girl that waited at table opened her being to the Lord and was immediately filled with the Holy Ghost and began to speak in tongues. All these 'big men stretched their necks and looked up to see what was happening and were saying, "Who is it?" Then they learned it was "the servant!" Nobody received but "the servant!" These things are hidden and kept back from the wise and prudent, but the little children, the lowly ones, are the ones that receive. We cannot have faith if we have honor one of another. A man who is going on with God won't accept honor from his fellow beings. God honors the man of a broken, contrite spirit. How shall I get there? So many people want to do great things, and to be seen doing them, but the one that God will use is the one that is willing to be hidden.

* How do we know who is truly heaven bound?

"Who is he that overcomes the world, but he that believeth that Jesus is the Son of God?" (1 John 5:5). God hath established the earth and humanity on the lines of faith. As you come into line, fear is cast out, the Word of God comes into operation and you find solid rock. The way to overcome is to believe Jesus is the Son of God. The commandments are all wrapped up in it.

When there is unity between you and God, the love of God is so real that you feel like you could do anything for Jesus, all the promises are yea and amen to those who believe. Your life is established in this realm. Always overcoming all that is in the world.

Who keeps the commandments? Those born of God. *"Ye are of God, little children, and have overcome them: because greater is he that is in you, than he that is in the world" (1 John 4:4)*. They that believe, love. When did He love us? When we were in the mire. What did He say? Thy sins are forgiven thee. Why did He say it? Because He loved us. What for? That He might bring many sons into glory. His object? That we might be with Him forever. All the pathway is an education for this high vocation and calling. This hidden mystery of love to us, the undeserving! For our sins the double blessing. *"...whatsoever is born of God overcomes the world: and this is the victory...even our faith" (1 John 5:4)*. He who believeth — to believe is to overcome. On the way to Emmaus Jesus, beginning from Moses and all the prophets, interpreted to them in all the Scriptures the things concerning Himself (Luke 24:27). He is the root! In Him is life. When we receive Christ, we receive God and the promises (Galatians 3:29), that we might receive the promise of the Spirit through faith. I am heir to all the promises because I believe. A great heir ship! I overcome because I believe the truth. The truth makes me free.

EXPERIENCES FROM THE AUTHOR

If I Was, I Am, If I Am, I Is!

While reading my Bible, I discovered Jesus Christ went about doing good and healing all who were sick and oppressed of the devil. I researched the subject in much greater detail. I studied and meditated on these truths and faith rose up in my heart. I discovered Isaiah 53.

Surely he hath borne our grief's, and carried our sorrows: yet we did esteem him stricken, smitten of God, and afflicted. But he was wounded for our transgressions, he was bruised for our iniquities: the chastisement of our peace was upon him; and with his stripes we are healed (Isaiah 53:4-5).

I found myself speaking out loud to my ears and commanded them to be open and normal. Then I spoke to my lungs and commanded them to be healed. Next I commanded my sinuses to be delivered so I could smell normal scents. The minute I spoke the Word of God to my physical man, my ears popped open. I was listening to Christian music during this time and the music became so loud that I had to turn it down. My lungs were clear, and I haven't experienced any lung congestion since. I used to be so allergic to dust that my mother had to work extra hard to keep our house dust-free. Dust has never come back to torment me or cause me problems. My sense of smell returned! I had broken my nose about four times due to fights, accidents, and rough activities. I could barely smell anything. Suddenly, I could smell a terrible odor. I tried to find out where it was coming from and then I looked at my feet and wondered if it could be them. I put my foot on a night stand and bent over toward it. I took a big sniff and nearly fell over. Man, did my feet stink! I went straight over to the bathroom and washed them in the sink.

Satanic Worshiper Delivered

One night I was witnessing in my dormitory room to three men. While sharing biblical truths with these three men, another man entered my room. We called him TJ. This individual had always been very different and strange. He was kind of out there. I had never even spoken to him up to that time, except one night when he showed a really nasty movie to the guys in his dorm. I had walked out of his room in disgust.

When TJ entered my room he began to preach some off-the-wall weird things about the devil. He said he was from California where he had been part of a satanic church. He showed us the ends of his fingers in which some of the ends were missing from the first joint out. He told us he had eaten them for power and drank human blood within satanic worship services. As he spoke, there seemed to be an invisible power speaking through him. He had come under the influence of a demonic presence, One of the guys who were in my room, Hussein, declared this was too much and left the room. The other two, Bobby and Willie, sat and listened.

I had never encountered anything as sinister and evil as this ever before. I honestly didn't know what to do at that time so I went downstairs to the barracks right below me. There was a fellow Christian I had the opportunity of working with who lived there. After I had given my heart to Jesus Christ, Willie, the cowboy, told me he was a born again, Spirit-filled Christian. I had yet to see the evidence of this in Willie's life but I didn't know where else to go. I knocked on Willie's door. When he opened the door I explained to him what happened in my room. He stepped into my dormitory and stopped. TJ was up on a wooden stool preaching under the power of the devil. Willie, turned tail and ran out of my room. He said he had no idea what to do and he couldn't handle this. He left me standing outside by my door.

I went back into my room and did the only thing I could - I cried out to Jesus. The minute I cried out, a bright light from heaven shone through my ceiling. I don't know if anyone else saw this bright light. All I know is what I needed to speak was placed within me. I began to preach Jesus to TJ! As I began to speak, the power of God fell in the room and TJ dropped to the floor, squirming and crawling like a snake. Willie and Bobby fell on their knees crying out to Jesus and gave their hearts to the Lord. I found myself kneeling over the top of TJ. I placed my hands upon him. Willie and Bobby came over and laid their hands upon him. With a voice of authority inspired by the Spirit, I commanded the demons to come out of the man. As God is my witness, three to five different voices came screaming out of TJ! After the demons were gone TJ gave his heart to Jesus Christ right then and there. All of these three men were filled with the Holy Ghost and spoke in tongues. The next Sunday they all went to church with me.

CHAPTER THREE

Sermon: Active Life of the Spirit-filled Believer

#30   I was on the water on route to Australia. We stopped at a place called Aden, where they were selling all kinds of ware. Among other things were some beautiful rugs and ostrich feathers in great quantities. There was a gentleman in "first class" who wanted feathers. He bought one lot and the next lot put up was too big; he did not want so many. He said to me, "Will you join me in buying these feathers?" I knew I did not want feathers for I had no room or use for them and I wouldn't know what to do with them if I did get them. However, he pleaded with me to join him. I perceived it was the Spirit that was directing me and I said, "Yes, I will." So the feathers were knocked down for fifteen dollars. Then I found the man had no money on him. He had plenty in his cabin. I perceived it was the Spirit again, so I paid for the feathers. He said to me, "I will get the money and give it to one of the stewards." I replied: "No, I'm sorry that were not do. I am known all over the ship so I want you to seek me out."

The man came to my cabin and brought the money. I said, "God wants me to talk to you. Please sit down." So he sat down and in ten minutes' time the whole of his life was completely changed, unraveled, broken up, so broken that like a big baby he wept and cried his way to salvation. It was "feathers" that did it. But you know we shall never know the mind of God till we learn to know the voice of God.

Smith - "Hard things are only opportunities to gain more glory for the Lord as He manifests His power. Every trial is a blessing in disguise.

#31   I will tell you what happened in Sydney, Australia. A man with a walking stick passed a friend and me. He had to get down and then twist over, and the tortures on his face made a deep impression on my soul. I asked myself, "Is it right to pass this man?" So I said to my friend, "There is a man in awful distress, and I cannot go any further. I must speak to him." I went over to this man and said to him, "You seem to be in great trouble." "Yes," he said, "I am in terrible shape and will be for the rest of my life." I said, "You see that hotel. Be in front of that door in five minutes and I will pray for you, and you shall be as straight as any man in in the world." This is a declaration of active faith in Jesus Christ. I came back after paying a bill, and sure enough he was there waiting for me. I will never forget him wondering if he was going to be trapped, or what was up that a man should stop him in the street and tell him he should be made straight. I had said it, so it must be. If you say or declare anything you must stand with God to make it so. Never say anything for bravado, without you having the authority or the right to say it. Always be sure of your foundation, and that you are honoring God. If there is anything about what you're doing to make you somebody, it will bring you sorrow. Your whole ministry will have to be on the line of humility, grace and blessing. We helped him up the two steps, passed him through to the elevator, and took him upstairs. It seemed difficult to get him from the elevator to my bedroom, as though Satan was making the last effort to take his life, but we got him there. Then in five minutes' time this man walked out of that bedroom as straight as any man has ever walked. He walked perfectly and declared he hadn't a pain in his body.

Smith - "I know that God's word is sufficient. One word from Him can change a nation. His word is from everlasting to everlasting. It is through the entrance of this everlasting Word, this incorruptible seed, that we are born again, and come into this wonderful salvation. Man cannot live by bread alone, but must live by every word that proceeded out of the mouth of God. This is the food of faith. "Faith cometh by hearing, and hearing by the Word of God."

#32   In a place in England I was teaching on the lines of faith and what would take place if we believed God. Many wonderful things were happening. When I was done teaching it appeared one man who worked in a coal mine had heard me. He was in trouble with a very stiff knee. He said to his wife, "I cannot help but think every day that that message of Wigglesworth's was to stir us to do something. I cannot get it out of my mind. All the men in the pit know how I walk with a stiff knee, and you know how you have wrapped it around with yards of flannel.

Well, I am going to act. You have to be the congregation." He got his wife in front of him. "I am going to act and do just as Wigglesworth did." He got hold of his leg unmercifully, saying, **"Come out, you devils, come out! In the name of Jesus.** Now, Jesus, help me. **Come out, you devils, come out."** Then he said, "Wife they are gone! Wife, they are gone. This is too good. I am going to act now." So he went to his place of worship and all the other coal workers were there. It was a prayer meeting. As he told them this story these men became delighted. They said, "Jack, come over here and help me." And Jack went. As soon as he was through in one home he was invited to another, delivering and losing these people of the pains they had gotten in the coal mine.

Smith - "Before God could bring me to this place He has broken me a thousand times. I have wept, I have groaned, I have travailed many a night until God broke me. It seems to me that until God has mowed you down you never can have this longsuffering for others. We can never have the gifts of healing and the working of miracles in operation only as we stand in the divine power that God gives us and we stand believing God, and having done all we still stand believing."

Sermon: Aflame for God

#33   I was traveling from Egypt to Italy. God was visiting me wonderfully on this ship, and every hour I was conscious of His blessed presence. A man on the ship suddenly collapsed and his wife was terribly alarmed, and everybody else was panicking. Some said that he was about to expire. But I saw it was just a glorious opportunity for the power of God to be manifested. Oh, what it means to be a flame of fire, to be indwelt by the living Christ! We are in a bad condition if we have to pray for power when an occasion like this comes along, or if we have to wait until we feel a sense of His presence. The Lord's promise was, "Ye shall receive power after that the Holy Ghost is come upon you," and if we will believe, the power of God will be always manifested when there is a definite need. When you exercise your faith, you will find that there is the greater power in you than that is in the world. Oh, to be awakened out of unbelief into a place of daring for God on the authority of His blessed Book and the redemptive work of Christ!

So right there on board that ship, in the name of Jesus I rebuked the devil, and to the astonishment of the man's wife and the man himself, he was able to stand. He said, "What is this? It is going all over me. I have never felt anything like this before." From the top of his head to the soles of his feet the power of God shook him. God has given us authority over all the power of the devil. Oh, that we may live in the place where we realize this always, and that were completely submitted to that authority!

Smith - It is an insult to ask God for power after you have received the baptism of the Holy Ghost. You have power! You have to ACT!

#34   Some years ago I was in Ceylon. In one place the folk complained, "Four days is not enough to be with us." "No," I said, "but it is a better than nothing." They said to me, "We are not touching the multitudes of people who are here." I said, "Can you have a meeting early in the morning, at eight o'clock?" They said they could and would if I so desired. So I said, "Tell all the mothers who want their babies to be healed to come, and all the people over seventy to come, and after that we hope to give an address to the people to make them ready for the Baptism in the Spirit."

It would have done you good to see the four hundred mothers coming at eight o'clock in the morning with their babies, and then to see the hundred and fifty old people, with their white hair, coming to be healed. We need to have something more than smoke and huff and puff to touch the people; we need to be a burning fire for God. His ministers must be flames of fire. In those days there were thousands out to hear the Word of God. I believe there were about three thousand persons crying for mercy at once that day. It was a great sight.

From that first morning on the meetings grew to such an extent that I would estimate every time some 5,000 to 6,000 gathered; and I had to preach in a temperatures of 110 degrees. Then I had to pray for these people who were sick. But I can tell you, a flame of fire can do anything. Things change in the fire. This was Pentecost. But what moved me more than anything else was this: there were hundreds who tried to touch me, they were so impressed with the power of God that was present. And many testified that with the touch they were healed, It was not that there was any virtue in me—the people's faith was exercised as it was at Jerusalem when they said Peter's shadow would heal them.

Smith - Be filled to overflowing with the Spirit. We are no good if we have only a full cup; we need to have an OVERFLOWING cup!

Sermon: After you have received power

#35   One day as I came into the house my wife said, "Which way did you come?" I answered that I had come in by the back way. "Oh," she said, "if you had come in by the front you would have seen a man there in a terrible state. There is a crowd of people around him and he is in terrible condition." Then the doorbell rang and she said, "There he is again. What shall we do?" I said, "Just be still." I rushed to the door and just as I was opening it the Spirit said, "This is what I baptized you for." I was very careful then in opening the door, and then I heard the man crying outside, "Oh I have committed the unpardonable sin, I am lost, I am lost."

I asked him to come in and when he got inside he said again

in awful distress, "I am lost, I am lost." Then the Spirit came upon me and I commanded the lying spirit to come out of the man in the name of Jesus. Suddenly he lifted up his arms and said, "I never did it." The moment the lying spirit was out of him he was able to speak the truth. I then realized the power in the Baptism of the Holy Spirit. It was the Spirit that said, "This is what I baptized you for," and I believe we ought to be in the place where we shall always be able to understand the mind of the Spirit amid all the other voices in the world.

Smith - Before a man can bind the enemy, he must know there is nothing binding him.

#36   One day as I was waiting for a taxi I stepped into a shoemaker's shop. I had not been there long when I saw a man with a green shade over his eyes, crying pitifully and in great agony. It was heart-rending and the shoemaker told me that the inflammation was burning out his eyes. I jumped up and went to the man and said, "You devil, come out of this man in the name of Jesus." Instantly the man said, "It is all gone, the pain has left and I can see now." That is the only Scriptural way, to touch the lives of people, and then preach afterwards. You will find as the days go by that the miracles and healings will be manifested. Because the Master was touched with the feeling of the infirmities of the multitudes they instantly gathered around Him to hear what He had to say concerning the Word of God. However, I would rather see one man saved than ten thousand people healed.

Smith - The resurrected Christ is there for you. Trust His presence. Trust His power. Trust His provision. He is alive for you!

#37 The other day we were going through a very thickly populated part of San Francisco when we noticed a large crowd gathered. I saw it from the window of the car and said I had to get out, which I did. There in the midst was a boy in the agonies of death. As I threw my arms around the boy I asked what the trouble was and he answered that he had terrible cramps. In the name of Jesus I commanded the devils to come out of him and at once he jumped up and not even taking time to thank me, ran off perfectly healed. We are God's own children, quickened by His Spirit and He has given us power over all the powers of darkness; Christ in us the open evidence of eternal glory, Christ in us the Life, the Truth, and the Way.

Smith - If you seek nothing but the will of God, He will always put you in the right place at the right time.

#38 When I was traveling from England to Australia I witnessed for Jesus, and it was not long before I had plenty of room all to myself. If you want a whole seat to yourself just begin to preach Jesus Christ. However, some people listened and began to be truly touched by God. One of the young men said to me, "I have never heard these truths before. You have so moved me that I must have a longer conversation with you." The young man told me that his wife was a great believer in Christian Science but was very sick now and although she had tried everything she had been unable to get relief, so she was seeing a doctor. But the doctor gave her no hope whatever. When her husband told her about me she became desperate because she was facing the realities of death and she asked that she might have an appointment to meet with me.

When I got to her I felt it would be unwise to say anything about Christian Science so I said, "You are in bad shape." She said, "Yes, the doctors give me no hope." I said, "I will not speak to you about anything but will just lay my hands upon you in the Name of Jesus and when I do you will be healed."

Immediately she was healed and that woke her up and she began to think seriously about her life. For three days she was lamenting over the things she might have to give up. "Will I have to give up the cigarettes?" "No," I said. "Will I have to give up the dance?" and again I replied "No." "Well, we have a little drinking sometimes and then we play cards also. Will I have to give—?" "No," I said, "you will not have to give up anything. Only let us see Jesus."

And right then she got such a vision of her crucified Savior and Jesus was made so real to her that she at once told her friends that she could not play cards any more, could not drink or dance any more, and she said she would have to go back to England to preach against this awful thing, called Christian Science. Oh, what a revelation Jesus gave her! Now if I had refused to go when called for, saying that I first had to go to my cabin and pray about it, I might have lost this opportunity for a precious woman to be healed and saved. After you have received the Holy Ghost you have power; you don't have to wait.

Smith - There are 4 principles we need to maintain: 1 READ the Word. 2 CONSUME the Word. 3 BELIEVE the Word. 4 ACT on the Word.

Bradford Convention, April 6, 1920

#39 I was asked to visit a man in a mental institution, a slave to alcoholism and nicotine. The evil power would not allow me to approach this man. But God gave me wonderful authority over the power of this evil spirit that was at work in him. Immediately God granted that a broken and contrite heart was given to him, and he was crying out for salvation. In just three short days he was out of that place. In the Name: of Jesus we dealt with the two evil powers—the hardest thing in life was to do without tobacco— but the mighty power of God came over him.

Smith - The future is not what you are going to be tomorrow. The future is what you are today.

#40   A woman in Paris suffered from epileptic fits for over 23 years and could not go out alone. She was instantly delivered healed and can now go out alone. The mother of this girl, too, was healed because of the testimony of her daughter.

Smith - God is more eager to answer than we are to ask.

#41   A young man, 27 years of age, was dumb. He came to a meeting sneering and laughing, and came very close to see what was going on. I thought he was seeking God, and put my hands on him. The power of God went through him. I said to him, "Shout, shout, shout!" and the people called out to him in his language, "Shout!" and for the first time in his life he began to shout. God gave him his speech even though he had been a mocker.

Smith - To the man of faith, there is not such a thing that is not an opportunity.

#42   Police in Switzerland. There were more people night after night seeking healing than there are attending this Convention. We were working until midnight. So many people were healed that two policemen were sent to apprehend me. They said I was doing it without credentials. The police wanted to see a wicked woman who had been healed of a rupture, and was the means of bringing others to be healed. When they heard this they said they wished all preachers did the same.

Smith - Do not think back, look back or act back.

#43   Multitudes of awful sinners were healed. A whole family (all wicked) was saved through being healed. Jesus is glorious. Surely He is the most lovely of all. Truly He was manifested to destroy the works of the devil. That Name manifests life as truly as ever it did.

Smith - **If you seek nothing but the will of God, He will always put you in the right place at the right time.**

#44 There was a woman with an awful distorted face (nose). I felt an awful sensation, as I do when I see cancer. I rebuked the disease in the Name of Jesus. The next night I forgot about the woman. She came to the meeting and when I saw her I said, "Oh, God! Oh, God!" The same nose shone like glass, and all the skin was new. Our God is a God of love. Who can describe His majesty and glory. Well might the poet say, "Crown Him with many crowns." We must do it. We must do it.

Smith - God wants your life to manifest His glory!

#45 There was a man with an incurable disease. The moment hands were laid on him he was perfectly healed, after 34 years of suffering from the work of Satan.

Smith - The Word of God is the food of faith.

#46 The presence of God was so gloriously manifested. A man on the railway was healed of a disease of 22 years. There was a wicked man healed. He was so broken in spirit that we had to break up the meeting till he got saved. He was going to tell everybody how he was saved. I tell you, there is something in healing. Like the man at the beautiful gate, when the people saw him leaping and praising God 5,000 were saved. God forbid we should glory in anything less than putting Jesus before anyone.

Smith - No wavering! A definite faith brings a definite experience and a definite utterance.

#47   I was taken to a place to see a girl whose bowels, the doctor said, were completely destroyed. No one could do anything for her. She was in a complete hopeless situation. Immediately she felt an inward power surging through her body as hands were laid upon her. She was gloriously healed by the power and the authority of the name of Jesus.

Smith - "If we've got what they got, then we can do what they did." - Polly Wigglesworth

#48   At one meeting there were 1,000 people extremely excited to hear the Word of God and about healing. God only knows how I have longed to see people saved, and God showed me in the spirit He would save. People put up their hands all over the place, as they wanted to be saved. Oh how wonderful it was to see how they flocked to God. God is the same God.

Smith - God wants to give you a faith that shakes hell!

#49   A woman came to be healed of a terrible cancer. How it did smell—but God healed her instantly. The husband got saved and the whole family with him. I believe there is a crown for all believers, but it will have to be fought for. There was a young woman vomiting blood. God awakened me in the middle of the night, and in the Name of Jesus I commanded the demon power to come out, and she was immediately healed. It is all in the precious name of Jesus Christ.

Smith - All of me, none of God. Less of me, more of God. None of me, all of God.

#50   At Zurich it was just the same. God worked amazing special miracles and wonders. The Holy Ghost is different to everyone else. *"The anointing ye have received abides within you."* There was a man with a disease you could not look at. I praise God for what Jesus does. In just ten minutes he was made whole. The man sat up in bed and said, "I know I am healed." The doctor came exactly at that time. He was amazed, and said to the man's wife, "Your husband is whole. Whatever has happened? It will not be necessary for me to come anymore." He had been attending his patient three times a day.

Smith - Discouraged one, cast your burden on the Lord. He will sustain you. Look unto Him and be lightened. Look unto Him now.

#51   A little boy four years of age was very ill. The doctor who had been attending him for several days said there was something terribly wrong with his brain. The Lord showed me the mischief was in the stomach area, so I laid hands on the child's stomach. A few hours later a worm, fifteen inches long, came out of his mouth, and the boy was made completely whole. Does God know? Hebrews 4:12-13. The discernment of God goes to every part of you—neither is there any creature not manifest in His sight.

Smith - I fail to see how you will ever reach a place where God will be able to use you until you get angry at the devil.

#52   In Ireland a woman had her thigh broken in two places. She lay in bed and could just reach the mantel-piece. When I laid hands on her she said, "It's going right down." "What is going right down?" "The power of God." And in His strength she arose from that bed of affliction completely healed in the name of Jesus.

Smith - There are boundless possibilities for you if you dare to believe.

Sermon: By faith

#53   I remember one night, being in the north of England and going around to see some sick people, I was taken into a house where there was a young woman lying on her bed, a very helpless case. Her reason was gone and many things were manifested that were absolutely Satanic, and I knew it.

She was a beautiful young woman. Her husband was quite a young man. He came in with a baby in his arms, leaned over and kissed his wife. The moment he did so she threw herself over on the other side of the bed, just as a lunatic would do, with no consciousness of the presence of her husband. It was heart-breaking, The husband took the baby and pressed the baby's lips to the mother. Again there was a wild frenzy. I said, to the sister who was attending her, "Have you anybody to help?" She answered, "We have done everything we could." I said, "Have you no spiritual help?" Her husband stormed and said, "Spiritual help? Do you think we believe in God after we have had seven weeks of no sleep and this maniac condition? If you think we believe in God, you are mistaken. You have come to the wrong house."

There was a young woman about eighteen who grinned at me as she passed out of the door, as much as to say, "You cannot do anything." But this brought me to a place of compassion for this poor young woman. And then with what faith I had I began to penetrate the heavens. I was soon out on the heights, and I tell you I never saw a man get anything from God who prayed on the earth level. If you get anything from God you will have to pray right into heaven, for all you want is there. If you are living an earthly life, all taken up with sensual things, and expect things from heaven, they will never come. God wants us to be a heavenly people, seated with Him in the heavenlies, and laying hold of all the things in heaven that are at our disposal.

I saw there, in the presence of that demented girl, limitations to my faith; but as I prayed there came another faith into my heart that could not be denied, a faith that grasped the promises, a faith that believed God's Word. I came from the presence of the glory back to earth. I was not the same man. I confronted the same conditions I had seen before, but in the name of Jesus. With a faith that could shake hell and move anything else, I cried to the demon power that was making this young woman a maniac, "Come out of her, in the name of Jesus!" She rolled over and fell asleep, and awakened in fourteen hours, perfectly sane and perfectly whole.

Smith - There is something about believing in God that makes God pass over a million people just to anoint you.

Sermon: Concerning Spiritual Gifts

#54   One young man who attended their meetings received the Baptism with the speaking in other tongues as the Spirit gave him utterance. The brethren were very upset about this and came to the father and said to him, "You must take your son aside and tell him to cease." They did not want anything to upset their meetings. The father told the son and said, "My boy, I have been attending this church for twenty years and have never seen anything of this kind. We are established in the truth and do not want anything new. We won't have it." The son replied, "If that is God's plan I will obey, but somehow or other I don't think it is." As they were going home the horse stood still; the wheels were in a deep rut. The father pulled at the reins but the horse did not move. He asked, "What do you think is up?" The son answered, "this carriage has become deeply established." God save us from becoming stationary.

Smith - God is always more willing to give than we are to receive. The trouble is, we do not ask Him for what He is more than willing to give us.

#55   I know a man who was full of the Holy Ghost and would preach only when he knew that he was mightily anointed by the power of God. He was asked to preach at a Methodist church. He was staying at the minister's house and he said, "You go on to the church service and I will follow." The place was packed with people but this man did not turn up and the Methodist minister, becoming anxious, so he sent his little girl to inquire why he had not come yet. As she came to the bedroom door she heard him crying out three times, "I will not go." She went back to her father and reported that she heard the man say three times that he would not go. The minister was troubled about it, but almost immediately after this the man came in, and, as he preached that night, the power of God was tremendously manifested. The preacher asked him, "Why did you tell my daughter that you were not coming?" He answered, "I know when I am filled. I am an ordinary man and I told the Lord that I dared not go and would not go until He gave me a fresh filling of the Spirit. The moment the glory filled me and overflowed I came to the meeting."

Smith - My Bible is my heavenly bank. I find everything I want in it.

#55   There is one thing I am very grateful to the Lord for, and that is that He has given me grace not to have a desire for money. The love of money is a great hindrance to many; and many a man is crippled in his ministry because he lets his heart run after financial matters. I was walking out one day when I met a godly man who lived opposite of my house and he said, "My wife and I have been talking together about selling our house and we feel constrained to sell it to you." As we talked together he persuaded me to buy his place, and before we said good-by I told him that I would take it. We always make big mistakes when we are in a hurry. I told my wife what I had promised, and she said, "How will you manage it?" I told her that I had managed things so far, but I did not know how I was going to keep this commitment. I somehow knew that I was out of God's divine order. But when a fellow gets out of divine order it seems that the last person he goes to is God himself. I was relying on an architect to help me, but that scheme fell through. I turned to my relations and I certainly had a mud on my face as one after another turned me down. I tried my friends and managed no better. My wife said to me, "Thou hast never been to God Yet." What could I do?

I have a certain place in our house where I go to pray. I have been there very often. As I went I said, "Lord, if you will get me out of this mess I got myself into, I will never trouble you on this line again." As I waited on the Lord He just gave me one word. It seemed a ridiculous thing, but it was the wisest counsel. There is divine wisdom in every word God speaks. I came down to my wife, saying, "What do you think? The Lord has told me to go to Brother Webster." I said, "It seems very ridiculous, for he is one of the poorest men I know." He was the poorest man I knew, but he was also the richest man I knew, for he knew God. My wife said, "Do What God says, and it will be right."

I went off at once to see him, and he said as he greeted me, "Smith, what brings you so early?" I answered, "The word of God." I said to him, "About three weeks ago I promised to buy a house of a man, and I am short 100 pounds ($500). I have tried to get this money, but somehow I seem to have missed God." "How is it," he asked, "that you have come to me only now?" I answered, "Because I went to the Lord about it only last night." "Well," he said, "it is a strange thing; three weeks ago I had 100 pounds. For years I have been putting money into a co-operative system and three weeks ago I had to go and draw 100 pounds out. I hid it under the mattress. Come with me and you shall have it. Take it. I hope it will bring as great a blessing to you as it has been a trouble to me." I had my word from God, and all my troubles were ended. This has been multiplied in a hundred ways since that time. If I had been walking along filled with the Holy Ghost, I would not have bought that house and would not have had all that pressure. I believe the Lord wants to deliver us from things of earth. But I am ever grateful for that word from God.

Smith - I am not moved by what I see or feel - but by what I believe!

Sermon: Dare to believe and to command

#56   A needy man came to me in a meeting. He was withered and wasted, in a hopeless condition; death lay in his eyes. He was so helpless he had to have someone on each side to carry him along. He said to me in a whisper, "Can you help me?"

This afflicted man, standing before me so helpless, so withered, he had had cancer of the stomach. The physicians had taken away the cancer from his stomach, but in removing it they had taken away the man's ability to swallow. The cancer was removed, and seemingly his life was spared, but he could not swallow any longer. In order to keep him from starving, they had made an opening in his stomach and inserted a tube about nine inches long, with a cup at the top, and he fed himself with liquids. For three months he had managed to keep alive, walking about like a skeleton. Here he was asking whether I could help him. What should I say? I remembered the promise, "If thou canst believe, all things are possible to him that believeth." And again, "He that believeth on me, the works that I do shall he do also; and greater works than these shall he do; because I go unto my Father."

The Word must be true. Jesus is with the Father, and therefore even greater works than His can be done if we believe. So I believed, and therefore I spoke.

"Go home and have a good supper," I said. The poor fellow replied, "I cannot swallow." I repeated, "On the authority of the

Word of God I say it. It is the promise of Jesus. Go home in the name of Jesus, and have a good supper." He went home. Supper was prepared. Many times before this he had taken food in his mouth and had been forced to spit it out again. But I had believed God. (I am here to inspire you.) I am a natural man, just as you are, but I dared to believe that he would swallow that night. So after he had filled his mouth with food, he chewed it, and then it went right down his throat. He ate until he was quite satisfied. He and his family went to bed filled with joy. The next morning when they arose they were filled with the same joy. Life had begun again, it seemed. The man looked down to see the opening which the physicians had made into his stomach, but it was gone. He did not need two openings, so when God opened the natural passage He closed the other. That is what God is like all the time. He brings things to pass when we believe and trust him. God wants you to realize this truth. Dare to believe, then dare to speak, and you shall· have whatsoever you say.

Smith - I am not here to entertain you, but to get you to the place where you can laugh at the impossible!

#57   A woman came up to me one night and asked, "do you think that I will be able to hear again?" She said, "I have had several operations, and the innards of my ears have been taken away. Is it possible for me ever to hear again?" I said, "If God has not forgotten how to make the innards for your ears you can hear again." Do you think God has forgotten? There is one thing God does forget—He forgets our sins when He forgives us—but He has not forgotten how to make the innards for ears. She went away rejoicing and hearing in the name of Jesus.

Smith - The willingness of God to answer prayer is much greater than the willingness of men to pray!

#58   A woman told me that her lungs were completely shredded, and that she could vomit up a pint of pus at any time. But when I invited people to receive divine healing, she stepped forward and dared to believe God, and she was completely healed in that very meeting by the power of Christ.

Smith - Drop the idea that you are so holy that God has got to afflict you with sickness. Sin is the cause of sickness, not righteousness!

#59   Not long ago I was in a meeting and the power of God was present in a remarkable way. I told the people that they could be healed without coming to the platform. I said that if they would rise and stand upon their feet wherever they were, I would pray and the Lord would heal them. There was a man who put up his hands. I said, "Can't that man rise?" They said he could not, so they lifted him up. We prayed, and that man was instantly healed then and there. His ribs had been broken and were not joined, but God healed him completely.

Smith - The way of faith is the Christ way. He wants to bringing us to a place where there is always an Amen in our hearts to the will of God.

#60 When it was evident that this crippled up man was healed, there was such faith throughout the congregation that a little girl said, "Please, gentleman, come to me." I could not see her, she was so small. The mother said, "My little girl wants you to come." So I went over to her. The girl was about fourteen years old, and she was a cripple. With tears running down her face, she asked, "Will you pray for me?" I said, "Will you dare to believe?" She answered, **"Oh, yes."** I prayed, and placed my hands on her head, in the name of Jesus. The girl said, "Mother, I am being healed. Take these leg braces off—take them all off." The mother loosed the straps and bands on the girl's legs. There was an iron on her foot about 3½ inches deep. She said, "Mother, I am sure I am healed. Take it all off." So her mother unstrapped the iron and took it off, and that girl began to walk up and down with total freedom. There was not a dry eyes in that place as the people saw that girl walk about with legs quite as true as when she was born. God had healed her right away. What did it? She dared to believe, and trusted God. "Please, gentleman, come to me," she had said. Her longing had been coupled with faith.

Smith - "Great faith is the product of great fights. Great testimonies are the outcome of great tests. Great triumphs can only come out of great trials."

TEACHING FROM SMITH WIGGLESWOTH

*Many Believers say they are in faith, but they are Lying to themselves!

There are many say they are believers but they are full of sickness and do not take hold of the life of the Lord Jesus Christ that is provided for them. I was taken to see a woman who was dying and said to her, "How are things with you?" She answered, "I have faith, I believe." I said, "You know that you do not have faith, you know that you are dying. It is not faith that you have, it is mere language." There is a difference between language and faith. I saw that she was in the hands of the devil. There was no possibility of life until he was removed from the premises. I hate the devil, and I laid hold of the woman and shouted, "Come out, you devil of death. I command you to come out in the name of Jesus." In one minute she stood on her feet in victory.

*There is a price you have to pay to move in the power of God!

Before God could bring me to this place He has broken me a thousand times. I have wept, I have groaned. I have travailed many a night until God broke me. It seems to me that until God has mowed you down you never can have this longsuffering and love for others. We can never have the gifts of healing and the working of miracles in operation only as we stand in the divine power that God gives us and we stand believing God. and having done all we still stand believing.

It is through the power of the Holy Ghost. You must not think that these gifts will fall upon you like ripe cherries. There is a sense in which you have to pay the price for everything you get. We must be covetous for God's best gifts, and say Amen to any preparation the Lord takes us through, in order that we may be humble, use able vessels through whom He Himself can operate by means of the Spirit's power.

EXPERIENCES FROM THE AUTHOR

I was Stabbed in the Face multiple times with a knife by a demon possessed women!

I drove my motorcycle to Oregon, stopping along the way to work on a fishing vessel. Then I drove my motorcycle up the Alcan Freeway, caught a ferry to Alaska, and finished driving to Anchorage.

After I arrived in Anchorage, it was quickened in my heart to stop at a small full gospel church that I used to visit. It just so happened that an evangelist I had known while I was in the Navy on Adak, Alaska, was there. We spent some time reminiscing what had happened the previous year. He shared how the Lord had laid upon his heart to go to Pennsylvania to open up an outreach center in a place called Mount Union, Pennsylvania. He invited me to go to Pennsylvania with him and his wife to open this evangelistic outreach. I perceived in my heart I needed to go with them. I planned to fly back to Wisconsin where he and his wife would pick me up as they went through. However, before I left Alaska the spirit of God had one more assignment for me: someone needed to be set free.

One Sunday we decided to attend a small church along the road to Fairbanks. I was the 1st to enter this little, old rustic church. When I went through the sanctuary doors I immediately noticed a strange, little elderly lady across from me sitting in the pews. She stared at me with the strangest look I have ever seen. I could sense immediately there was something demonic about her. Out of the blue this little lady jumped up, got out of the pew, and ran out of the church. I perceived that God wanted me to go minister to her.

After the service, I asked the pastor who the elderly lady was who ran out of the service. He said she was not a member of his church but she came once in a great while. He said she and her husband lived in a run-down house on a dirt road. I asked if it would be okay to go and see her. He said he had no problems with this, especially since she wasn't a part of his church. We followed the directions the pastor gave us. When we arrived at this lady's house we found it exactly as the pastor had said. It was a rundown house with its yard overflowing with old furniture and household items. I don't know how they could survive the winters in Alaska in such a poorly-built house. As we got out of the car, a little old man met us outside. It was her husband. He was thanking God as he walked toward us and said he knew we were men of God and had been sent to help his poor wife.

We went to the house having to go down the twisting cluttered filled path. We entered through a screen door that led into their kitchen. When we entered the kitchen we could see his wife over at a utility sink. Her back was to us but we could see she was peeling carrots over her kitchen sink with a very large butcher knife. She turned to face us as I began to speak to her. I could hardly believe my eyes! This little lady's eyes were glowing red. Fear tried to fill my heart as she looked at me with the big knife, a butcher's knife in her hand. Immediately I came against the spirit of fear in my mind quoting the Scripture *"God has not given me the spirit of fear but of power love and a sound mind"*

I began to share with her about Jesus. The next thing I knew she was coming right at me with her knife as if she was filled with great rage. The knife was still in her hand when she spun around. I hadn't seen her drop it. The next thing I knew she was hitting me in the face very hard. As she was hitting me in the face out of my mouth came **In the Name of Jesus!**

The minute I came against this attack in the name of Jesus, she literally was picked up by an invisible power and flew across the room about 10 feet or more. She slammed against the bare wall and slipped down to the floor. Amazingly when she hit the wall she was not hurt. I went over to her continuing to cast the demons out of her. Once she was free she told us her story. Her uncle had repeatedly molested and raped her when she was very young girl. She thought she was free from him when he got sick and died. But then he began to visit her from the dead, continuing to molest and rape her at night. To her it was physical and real. She did not know it was a familiar spirit disguised as her uncle. I led her to the Lord. Her and her husband began to go to church with us until I left Alaska.

Years later the evangelist who was with me heard me retell this story at a church and said I was not telling it correctly. I wondered if he thought I was exaggerating. He said that he was actually standing behind me while she was slapping me. But it wasn't her hand she was slapping me with, she had been stabbing me in the face with her knife repeatedly. He said he knew that I was a dead man because nobody could survive being stabbed in the face repeatedly with a large butcher knife. I did feel something hit my face but I thought it was her hand. Instead it was her knife and it could not pierce my skin! Thank God for his love and his mercy.

Deliverance to the Captives

#61   After I had received the Baptism of the Holy Ghost (and I know that I received; for the Lord gave me the Spirit in just the same way as He gave Him to the disciples at Jerusalem), I sought the mind of the Lord as to why I was baptized. One day I came home from work and went into the house and my wife asked me, "Which way did you come in?" I told her that I had come in at the back door. She said, "There is a woman upstairs and she has brought an old man of eighty to be prayed for. He is raving up there and a great crowd is outside the front door, ringing the door-bell and wanting to know what is going on in the house." The Lord quietly whispered, "This is what I baptized you for."

I carefully opened the door of the room where the man was, desiring to be obedient to what my Lord would say to me. The man was crying and shouting in distress, "I am lost! I am lost! I have committed the unpardonable sin. I am lost! I am lost!" My wife said, "Dad, what shall we do?" The Spirit of the Lord moved me to cry out, "Come out, thou lying spirit." In a moment the evil spirit went, and the man was free. Deliverance to the captives! And the Lord said to me, "This is what I baptized you for.

Smith - "Repeat in your heart often: "baptized with the Holy Ghost and fire, fire, fire!" All the unction, and weeping, and travailing comes through the baptism of fire, and I say to you and say to myself, purged and cleansed and filled with renewed spiritual power." *"Who makes his ministers a flame of fire." Heb. 1:7*

#62   I was traveling one day in a railway train in Sweden. At one station there boarded the train an old lady with her daughter. The old lady's expression was so troubled that I enquired what was the matter with her. I heard that she was going to the hospital to have her leg taken off. She began to weep as she told that the doctors had said there was no hope for her except through having her leg amputated. She was seventy years old. I said to my interpreter, "Tell her that Jesus can heal her." The instant this was said to her, it was as though a veil was taken off her face, it became so light. We stopped at another station and the carriage filled up with people. There was a rush of men to board that train and the devil said, "You're done for now. There's no way you can pray with all of these people here" But I knew I had God working with me, for hard things are always opportunities to give the Lord more glory when He manifests His power. Every trial is a blessing.

There have been times when I have been pressed through circumstances and it seemed as if a dozen road engines were going over me, but I have found that the hardest things are just the right opportunities for the grace of God to work. We have such a lovely Jesus. He always proves Himself to be such a mighty Deliverer. He never fails to plan the best things for us.

The train began moving and I crouched down, and in the name of Jesus commanded the disease to leave. The old lady cried, "I'm healed. I know I'm healed." She stamped her leg and said, "I'm going to prove it." So when we stopped at another station she marched up and down, and shouted, "I'm not going to the hospital." Once again our wonderful Jesus had proven Himself a Healer of the broken-hearted, a Deliverer of one that was bound.

Smith - "Wherever the Holy Ghost has right of way, the gifts of the Spirit will be in manifestation; and where these gifts are never in manifestation, I question whether He is present."

#63   At one time I was so bound that no human power could help me. My wife was looking for me to pass away. There was no help. At that time I had just had a faint glimpse of Jesus as the Healer. For six months I had been suffering from appendicitis, occasionally getting temporary relief. I went to the mission of which I was pastor, but I was brought to the floor in terrible and awful agony, and they brought me home to my bed. All night I was praying, pleading for deliverance, but none came. My wife was sure it was my home call and sent for a physician. He said that there was no possible chance for me-my body was too weak. Having had the appendicitis for six months, my whole system was drained, and, because of that, he thought that it was too late for an operation. He left my wife in a state of broken-heartedness.

After he left, there came to our door a young man and an old lady. I knew that she was a woman of real prayer. They came upstairs to my room. This young man jumped on the bed and commanded the evil spirit to come out of me. He shouted, *"Come out, you devil; I command you to come out in the name of Jesus!"* There was no chance for an argument, or for me to tell him that I would never believe that there was a devil inside of me. The thing had to go in the name of Jesus, and it went, and I was instantly healed.

I arose and dressed and went downstairs. I was still in the plumbing business, and I asked my wife, "Is there any work in? I am all right now, and I am going to work." I found there was a certain job to be done and I picked up my tools and went off to do it. Just after I left, the doctor came in, put his hat down in the hall, and walked up to the bedroom. But the invalid was not there. "Where is Mr. Wigglesworth ?" he asked. "Oh, doctor, he's gone out to work," said my wife. "You'll never see him alive again," said the doctor; "they'll bring him back a corpse."

Well, I'm the corpse. Since that time, in many parts of the world, the Lord has given me the privilege of praying for people with appendicitis; and I have seen a great many people up and dressed within a quarter of an hour from the time I prayed for them. We have a living Christ who is willing to meet people on every line.

Smith - People search everywhere today for things with which they can heal themselves & ignore the fact that the Balm of Gilead is within easy reach

#64   A number of years ago I met Brother D. W. Kerr and he gave me a letter of introduction to a brother in Zion City named Cook. I took his letter to Brother Cook, and he said, "God has sent you here." He gave me the addresses of six people and asked me to go and pray for them and meet him again at 12 o'clock. I got back at about 12:30 and he told me about a young man who was to be married the following Monday. His sweetheart was in Zion City dying of appendicitis. I went to the house and found that the physician had just been there and had pronounced that there was no hope. The mother was nearly out of her mind and was pulling her hair, and saying, "Is there no deliverance!" I said to her,

"Woman, believe God and your daughter will be healed and be up and dressed in fifteen minutes." But the mother just went on screaming.

They took me into the bedroom, and I prayed for the girl and commanded the evil spirit to depart in the name of Jesus. She cried, "I am healed." I said to her, "Do you want me to believe that you are healed? If you are healed, get up." She said, "You get out of the room, and I'll get up." In less than ten minutes the doctor came in. He wanted to know what had happened. She said, "A man came in and prayed for me, and I'm healed." The doctor pressed his finger right in the place that had been so sore, and the girl neither moaned nor cried. He said, **"This is God."** It made no difference whether he acknowledged it or not, I knew that God had worked. Our God is real in saving and healing power today. Our Jesus is just the same, yesterday, and today, and forever. He saves and heals today just as of old, and He wants to be your Savior and your Healer.

Smith - There must come up from us a cry that cannot be satisfied with anything but God.

#65   I was once at an afternoon meeting. The Lord had been graciously with us and many had been healed by the power of God. Most of the people had gone home and I was left alone, when I saw a young man who was evidently hanging back to have a word. I asked, "What do you want?" He said, "I wonder if I could ask you to pray for me." I said, "What's the trouble?" He said, "Can't you smell?" The young fellow had gone into sin and was suffering the consequences. He said, "I have been turned out of two hospitals. I am broken out all over. I have abscesses all over me." And I could see that he had a bad breaking out at the nose. He said, "I heard you preach, and could not understand about this healing business, and was wondering if there was any hope for me."

I said to him, "Do you know Jesus?" He did not know the first thing about salvation, but I said to him, "Stand still." I placed my hands on his head and then on his clothes which were over the top of his loins and cursed that terrible disease in the name of Jesus. He cried out, "I know I'm healed. I can feel a warmth and a glow all over me." I said, "Who did it?" He said, "Your prayers." I said, "**No, it was Jesus!**" He said, "Was it He? **Oh, Jesus! Jesus! Jesus**, save me." And that young man went away healed and saved. Oh, what a merciful God we have! What a wonderful Jesus is ours!

Smith - I can get more out of believing God for one minute than I can by shouting at Him all night.

Faith in the living word

#66   Every day I live I am more and more convinced that very few who are saved by the grace of God have the divine revelation of how great is their authority over darkness, demons, death and every power of the enemy by the name of Jesus Christ. It is a real joy when we realize our inheritance on this line.

I was speaking like this one day, and someone said, "I have never heard anything like this before. How many months did it take you to put together this sermon?" I said, "Brother, God impress upon my wife from time to time to get me to preach, and I promised her I would. I used to labor hard for a week to get a message together. I would simply give out my text and then sit down and say, 'I am done.' O brother, I have given up getting the messages together anymore. They all come down from heaven, and the sermons that come down as He wants them. Then they go back to God, with much results in fruit, for the Word of God declares that His Word shall not return unto Him void. If you get anything from God, it will be fresh from heaven. But these messages were also transform you as you speak them.

Smith - Every new revelation brings a new dedication.

Sermon: Gifts of Healings, and Miracles

#67   In a meeting a young man stood up, a pitiful object, with a face full of sorrow.

I said, "What is it, young man?" He said he was unable to work, because he could barely walk. He said, "I am so helpless. I have consumption and a weak heart, and my body is full of pain."

I said, "I will pray for you." I said to the people, "As I pray for this young man, I want you to look at his face and see it change."

As I prayed his face changed and there was a wonderful transformation. I said to him, now "Go out and run a mile and come back to the meeting."

He came back and said, "I can now breathe freely."

These meetings continuing but I did not seem any longer. After a few days I saw him again in the meeting. I said, "Young man, tell the people what God has done for you."

"Oh," he said, "I have been back to work. I bought some papers to sell and I have made $4.50." Praise God, this wonderful stream of salvation never runs dry. You can take a deep drink, it is close to you. It is a river that is running deep and there is plenty for all who are thirsty.

Smith - You will do more in one year if you are really filled with the Holy Ghost than you could do in fifty years apart from Him.

#68   In a meeting a man rose and said, "Will you touch me, I am in a terrible way. I have a family of children, and through an accident in the in the coal mines and I have had no work for two years. I cannot open my hands."

I was full of sorrow for this poor man and something happened which had never come before. We are in the infancy of this wonderful outpouring of the Holy Spirit and there is so much more for us. I put out my hand, and before my hands reached his, he was loosed and made perfectly free.

Smith - Wigglesworth once told a woman he had a cure for sickness in his bag. When asked to show it, he says 'I opened my bag & took out my Bible.

#69   Once a woman stood up in one of our meetings asking for prayer. I prayed for her and she was instantly healed. She cried out, "It is a miracle! It is a miracle! It is a miracle!" That is what God wants to do for every one of us all the time. As soon as we get free in the Holy Ghost something will happen.

Smith - Don't ever indulge in unprofitable conversation. Feed on the Word of God.

Sermon: Full! Full! Full!

#70   For many years the Lord has been taking me from glory to glory and keeping me from spiritual stagnation. When I was in the Wesleyan Methodist Church I was sure I was saved and was sure I was all right. The Lord said to me, "Come out," and I came out. When I was with the people known as the Brethren I was sure I was all right now. But the Lord said, "Come out." Then I went into the Salvation Army. At that time it was full of life and there were revivals everywhere. But the Salvation Army went into natural things and the great revivals that they had in those early days ceased. The Lord said to me, "Come out," and I came out. I have had to come out three times since. I believe that this Pentecostal revival that we are now in is the best thing that the Lord has on the earth today, and yet I believe that God has something out of this that is going to be still much better. God has no use for any man who is not hungering and thirsting for yet more of Himself and His righteousness.

Smith - To live two days in succession on the same spiritual plane is a tragedy.

#71 When you deal with a cancer case, recognize that it is a living evil spirit that is trying to destroy the victim's body and snuff out their life. I had to pray for a woman in Los Angeles one time who was suffering with cancer, and as soon as it was cursed it stopped bleeding. It was dead. The next thing that happened was that the natural body expelled it because the natural body had no room for dead matter. It came out like a great big ball with tens of thousands of fibers. All these fibers had been pressing into the flesh. These evil powers move to get further hold of the system, but the moment they are destroyed their hold is gone. Jesus said to His disciples that He gave them power to loose and power to bind. It is our privilege in the power of the Holy Ghost to loose the prisoners of Satan and to let the oppressed go free.

Smith - I don't often spend more than half an hour in prayer - but I never go more than half an hour without praying

#72 I was called to a certain town in Norway. The hall seated approximately 1500 people. When I got to the place it was packed to the roof, and hundreds were trying to get in. There were some policemen there. The first thing I did was to preach to the people outside the building. Then I said to the policemen, "It hurts me very much that there are more people outside than inside and I feel I must preach to the people. I would like you to get me the market place to preach in." They secured for me a great park and a big stand was erected and I was able to preach to thousands. After the preaching we had some amazing cases of healing. One man came a hundred miles bringing his food with him. He had not been passing anything through his stomach for over a month as he had a great cancer in his stomach. He was healed instantly at that meeting, and opening his parcel, he began eating before all the people. There was a young woman there with a stiff hand. Instead of the mother making the child use her arm she had allowed the child to keep the arm dormant until it was stiff, and she had grown up to be a young woman and was like the woman that was bowed down with the spirit of infirmity. As she stood before me I cursed the spirit of infirmity in the name of Jesus. It was instantly cast out and the arm was free. Then she waved it all over. At the close of the meeting the devil laid out two people with epileptic fits, When the devil is manifesting himself, then is the time to deal with him. Both of these people were wonderfully delivered, and they both stood up and thanked and praised the Lord. What a wonderful time we had.

Smith - We must not be content with a mere theory of faith. We must have faith within us so that we move from the ordinary into the extraordinary

TEACHING FROM SMITH WIGGLESWOTH

* How does Satan get an opening into a believers life?

When the saint ceases to seek after holiness, purity, righteousness, truth; when he ceases to pray, stops reading the Word and gives way to carnal appetites, then it is that Satan comes. So often sickness comes as a result of disobedience. David said, "Before I was afflicted, I went astray." Seek the Lord and He will sanctify every thought, every act, till your whole being is ablaze with holy purity and your one desire will be for Him who has created you in holiness. Oh, this holiness! Can we be made pure? We can. Every inbred sin must go. God can cleanse away every evil thought. Can we have a hatred for sin and a love for righteousness? Yes, God will create within thee a pure heart. He will take away the stony heart out of the flesh. He will sprinkle thee with clean water and thou shalt be cleansed from all thy filthiness. When will He do it? When you seek Him for such inward purity.

* This is the day of purifying.

This is the day of holiness. This is the day of separation. This is the day of waking. O God, let us wake today! Let the inner spirit wake into consciousness that God is calling us. The Lord is upon us. We see that the day is upon us. We look at the left side, we look at the right side, we see everywhere new theories. New things will not stand the light of the truth When you see these, things, you know that there must be a great falling away before the day And it is coming. It is upon us.

EXPERIENCES FROM THE AUTHOR

How God Miraculously Healed My Broken Back

In the winter of 1977, I was working at the Belleville Feed and Grain Mill. My job was to pick up the corn, wheat, and oats from the farmers, and bring it to the mill. There it would be mixed and combined with other products for the farmers' livestock.

One cold, snowy day, the owner of the feed mill told me to deliver a load of cattle feed to an Amish farm. It was an extremely bad winter that year, with lots of snow. I was driving an International 1600 Lodestar. I backed up as far as I could to this Amish man's barn without getting stuck. The Amish never had their lanes plowed in those days, and they most likely still do not. I was approximately seventy-five feet away from his barn, which meant that I had to carry the bags at least seventy-five feet. I think there were about eighty bags of feed, with each bag weighing approximately one hundred pounds. During those years I only weighed about 130 pounds. I would carry one bag on each of my shoulders, stumbling and pushing my way through the heavy, deep snow to get up the steep incline into the barn. Then I would stack the bags in a dry location. As usual, nobody came out to help me. Many a time when delivering things to the farms, the Amish would watch me work without lending a helping hand. About the third trip, something frightening happened to me as I was carrying two one-hundred-pound bags upon my shoulders. I felt the bones in my back snap. Something drastic just happened. I fell to the ground at that very moment almost completely crippled. I could barely move. I was filled with intense overwhelming pain.

I had been spending a lot of my time meditating in the Word of God. Every morning, I would get up about 5:00 a.m. to study. I had one of those little bread baskets with memorization scriptures in it. I believe you can still buy them to this day at a Christian bookstore. Every morning I would memorize from three to five of them. It would not take me very long, so all day long I would be meditating on these verses.

The very minute I fell down, immediately I cried out to Jesus, asking him to forgive me for my pride, and for being so stupid in carrying two hundred pounds on my little frame. After I asked Jesus to forgive me, I commanded my back to be healed in the name of Jesus Christ of Nazareth. Since I believed I was healed, I knew that I had to act now upon my faith. Please understand that I was full of tremendous pain, but I had declared that I was healed by the stripes of Jesus. The Word of God came out of my mouth as I tried to get up and then fell back down.

Even though the pain was more intense than I can express, I kept getting back up speaking the name of Jesus, then I would fall back down again. I fell down more times than I can remember. After some time I was able to take a couple steps, then I would fall again. This entire time I was saying, "In the name of Jesus, in the name of Jesus, in the name of Jesus." I finally was able to get to the truck. I said to myself if I believe I'm healed then I will unload this truck in the name of Jesus. Of course, I did not have a cell phone in order to call for help and the Amish did not own any phones on their property. Now, even if they would have had a phone, I would not have called for help. I had already called upon my help, and His name was Jesus Christ. I knew in my heart that by the stripes of Jesus I was healed. I then pulled a bag off of the back of the truck, with it falling on top of me. I would drag it a couple feet, and then fall down.

Tears were running down my face as I spoke the Word of God over and over. By the time I was done with all of the bags, the sun had already gone down. Maybe six or seven hours had gone by. I painstakingly pulled myself up into that big old 1600 Lodestar. It took everything within me to shift gears, pushing in the clutch, and driving it. I had to sit straight like a board all the way.

I finally got back to the feed mill late in the evening. Everybody had left for home a long time ago with the building being locked up. I struggled out of the Lodestar and stumbled and staggered over to my Ford pickup. I got into my pickup, and made it back to the converted chicken house. I went back to my cold, unheated, plywood floor room. It took everything in me to get my clothes off. It was a very rough and long night.

The next morning when I woke up, I was so stiff that I could not bend in the least. I was like a board. Of course, I was not going to miss work, because by the stripes of Jesus I was healed. In order to get out of bed, I had to literally roll off the bed, hitting the floor. Once I had hit the floor, it took everything for me to push myself back up into a sitting position. The tears were rolling down my face as I put my clothes and shoes on, which in itself was a miracle. I did get to work on time, though every step was excruciatingly painful. Remember, I was only twenty-one at the time, but I knew what faith was and what it wasn't. I knew that I was healed no matter how it looked, that by the stripes of Jesus Christ I was healed.

When I got to work I did not tell my boss that I had been seriously hurt the day before. I walked into the office trying to keep the pain off of my face. For some reason he did not ask me what time I made it back to work. I did not tell him to change the time clock for me in order to be paid for all of the hours I was out on the job. They had me checked out at the normal quitting time. (The love of money is what causes a lot of people not to get healed.) My boss gave me an order for feed that needed to be delivered to a local farmer. If you have ever been to a feed and grain mill, you know that there is a large shoot where the feed comes out. After it has been mixed, you have to take your feed bag, and hold it up until it's filled. It creates tremendous strain on your arms and your back, even if you're healthy. As I was filling the bag, it almost felt like I was going to pass out, because I was in tremendous pain. Now, I'm simply saying, "In the name of Jesus, in the name of Jesus, in the name of Jesus" under my breath. The second bag was even more difficult than the first bag, but I kept on saying, "In the name of Jesus." I began on the third bag and as I was speaking the name of Jesus, the power of God hit my back and I was instantly and completely, totally healed from the top of my head, to the tip of my toes. I was healed as I went on my way. My place of employment never did know what had happened to me. That has been 38 years ago. And I'm still healed by the stripes of Christ.

Abused Beat up Woman Instantly Healed!

I had to go to a local business place and as I was getting ready to go in, there was a precious African-American lady who was moving really slow. She got to the entrance and there was step up. It was only approximately 4 or 6 inches high. She could not even lift her foot that high. I asked her what was wrong and she informed me that her ex-boyfriend and his buddy had beaten her up the night before. She was bruised, black and blue and stiff from head to toe and could barely move any part of her body.

The Lord had been speaking to me about releasing His power through the spoken word. He had Quicken to my heart that I should leave every word that I spoke would come to pass. That Moses and Samuel had come tool the place were not one word they spoke fell to the ground. And that if I would believe the Scriptures, that said we would give an account of every word we speak, and only speak that which you desire to happen according to the will of the father, it would come to pass.

This particular lady turned her back on me as she tried to continue to lift her foot. At that moment, it was quickened in my heart to speak to her body. There was another gentleman standing there waiting to also enter this building. Without even thinking I pointed my finger at her body towards her back and commanded that in the name of Jesus Christ of Nazareth that all of her afflictions, pains and bruising of the beating to be instantly gone in the name of Jesus. I did not shout or speak loud. I simply spoke it at a normal voice. The minute I spoke I perceived that the spirit of God literally hit her body. Instantly, her foot came up real high as if something had been holding it down but now sprang forth being connected to a bungee cords.

She started moving both of her legs and her feet up and down very rapidly. She spun around and stared at me. This may sound strange but she was as white as a sheet (whatever that means). lol

She asked me with a very astonished quivering, mystified and almost in an angry voice, what just happened to me. I preached Jesus Christ and ministered the truth to her. She was still standing there under the power of God as I left.

The gentleman who was right behind me stood there watching all of this. I think he was so strong with amazement that he himself could not say anything!

CHAPTER FIVE

God working in Switzerland

#73   Everything I have seen in Switzerland has brought me to a place of brokenness before God. At Bern I have stood in a place which has been packed with a multitude of people. I sold moved by God that I ended up weeping as I have seen the needs of the people and then God gave us victory. Hundreds have been saved by the power of God. At Neuchatel God was working marvelously and the devil worked in between, but God is greater than all the Devils and the demons combined together. At my second visit to Neuchatel the largest theater was hired and it was packed, and God moved upon the people, and on an average 100 souls were saved each night, and many healed through God's touch, yet many did not have the Pentecostal teaching, and one man actually had meetings in opposition at places, but who Is the man who dares to put his hand on the child of God? This man also had prayer meetings to try to prevent people from going to the meetings, but they all turned to nothing but confusion. People came to be ministered   to.

Smith - "To discern spirits we must dwell with Him who is holy, and He will give the revelation and unveil the mask of Satanic power on all lines."

#74 The Holy Ghost is preparing us for some wonderful event. I feel a burning in my bones. I preached one night on Eph. 3 for 3½ hours, and so powerful was the Word that the people did not seem inclined to move. I preached and prayed with the sick until 11:30 p.m. Four people brought a man who was paralyzed and blind; the power of God fell upon him and us and he now walks and sees and is praising God. I have not been to one meeting where the power of God has not been upon us. I say this to His glory.

Smith - I cannot understand God by impressions or feelings. I cannot get to know God by sentiments. I am going to know Him by His Word.

#75 At Bern there is a band of praying people. Truly we have seen wonderful things. A girl was brought to me sitting in a chair. I would not minister at first, but told her she must wait and hear the Word of God. Her mother who had come with her was greatly moved as she listened to God's Word being expounded. I then laid hands on the girl, who had never walked. The power of God worked and she now walks. Another case, where a man had had a cancer taken out of his neck, after which he could no longer eat, not being able to swallow. He told me he could not even swallow the juice of a cherry. He had a pipe inserted in his neck so that food could be poured through it into his stomach. I said to him, "You will eat tonight." I prayed with him. He came the next day. I saw that the color had come back into his face, and he told me he had been eating, and could swallow comfortably. He had looked for the hole where the pipe had been inserted in his neck but could not find It. God had completely healed him. He was well known; he was a tea grower and people said he had come to life again. When the Son of God touches a man he does come to life.

Smith - God's plan is always this; if you will believe, you shall see the glory of God!

#76 A man came to me suffering from diabetes. The power of God was upon me and I realized that God was working upon this man. I said God has healed you. We took his address and then we checked up on him. He went to the doctor to be examined because he knew he was healed and asked him to examine him. He did so and stated that he was unable to find any trace of the disease whatever. He asked the doctor to give him a certificate which he did and I personally saw it.

Smith - Oh for a simple faith to receive all that God so lavishly offers!

#77 A young woman was dying of consumption, and her doctor had given her up. I laid hands on her in the name of Jesus and immediately she knew that the disease had passed from her body. This girl went to the doctor, who examined her and said, "Whatever has taken place, you have no consumption now." She replied, "Doctor I have been prayed over; can I tell the people I am healed?" And he said, "Yes, and that I could not heal you." "If I am to tell will you put it in black and white?" And he gave her a certificate which I saw. God had healed her.

Smith - You are in a great place when you have no-one to turn to but God.

#78 A man was brought into one of the meetings in a wheel chair. He could not walk except by the aid of two sticks, and even then his locomotion was very slow. I saw him in that helpless condition, and told him about Jesus Christ. Oh, that wonderful name! Glory to God! "They shall call His name Jesus." I placed my hands upon his head and said, "In the name of Jesus thou art made whole." This helpless man cried out "It is done, it is done, Glory to God, it is done!" And he walked out of the building perfectly healed. The man who brought him in the wheel chair and the children said that father so and so Is walking. Praise the Lord He is the same yesterday, today and forever.

Smith - God rejoices when we manifest a faith that holds Him to His word.

Sermon: Great Grace Upon the Church

#79   I have had some wonderful times in Belfast, Ireland, and in fact all over Ireland. I was in Belfast one day when a young man approached me and said: "Brother Wigglesworth, I am very much distressed," and he told me why. They had an old lady in their assembly who used to pray heaven down upon them. She had an accident. Her thigh was broken and they took her away to the infirmary. They put her in a plaster of Paris cast and she was in that condition for five months. Then they broke the cast and lifted her on to her feet and asked her to walk. She fell again and broke her leg in another place. To their dismay they discovered that the first break had never knitted together. They brought her home and laid her on the couch and the young man asked me to go and pray for her. When I got into the house I asked: "Do you believe that God can heal you?" She said "Yes. When I heard you had come to the city I thought, 'This is my chance to be healed.'

"An old man, her husband, was sitting in a chair, had been sitting there for four years; helpless. And he said : "I do not believe. I will not believe. She was the only help I had. She has been taken away with a broken leg, and they have brought her back with her leg broken twice. How can I believe God?"

I turned to her and said: "Now is this correct? Yes," she said, "it is the truth." The right leg was broken in two parts. Physicians can join up bones beautifully, and make them fit together, but if God doesn't come in with His healing power, there is no physician who can heal them. As soon as the oil was placed upon her head and hands laid on, instantly down the right limb there was a stream of life, and she knew it. She said: "I am healed." I said: "If you are healed, you do not need anybody to help you." So I left the room. Immediately after I left she took hold of the mantle shelf above her head and pulled herself up and walked all around the room. She was perfectly healed.

The old man said: "Make me walk." I said: "You old sinner, repent." Then he began: "You know, Lord, I didn't mean it." I really believe he was in earnest, and to show you the mercy and compassion of God, the moment I laid hands upon him, the power of God went thru him and he rose up after four years being in that chair and walked around the room. That day both he and his wife were made whole.

Smith - The resurrected Christ is there for you. Trust His presence. Trust His power. Trust His provision. He is alive for you!

SERMON: Greater Works than These

#80   I was having some meetings in Belfast, and this is the rising tide of what I believe was the move of the Spirit in a certain direction, to show the greatness of that which was to follow. Night after night the Lord had led me on certain lines of truth. There was so much in it that people did not want to go home, and every night until ten o'clock we were opening up the Word of God. They came to me and said: "Brother, we have been feasting and are so full we are we are about ready to burst. Don't you think it is time to call an altar service?"

I said I knew that God was working and the time would come when the altar service would be called, but we would have to get the mind of the Lord upon it. There was nothing more said. They began early in the afternoon to bring the sick people. We never had a thing said about it. The meeting came and every seat was taken up, the window sills were filled and every nook and corner. The glory of God filled the place. It was the easiest thing in the world to preach; it came forth like a river, and the power of God rested mightily upon everyone. There were a lot of people who had been seeking the baptism of the Holy Ghost for years. Sinners were in the meeting, and sick people. What happened? God hears me say this: There was a certain moment in that meeting when every sick person was healed, every lame person was healed, and every sinner saved, and it all took place in five minutes. There comes into a meeting sometimes something we cannot understand, and it is amazing how God shows up.

Smith - It is God's delight to make possible to us that which seems impossible.

#81   I want all you people to totally delivered, all to be filled with peace, all to be without pain or sickness, I want all to be free. There is a man here with great pain in his head, I am going to lay my hands on him in the name of Jesus and he shall tell you what God has done, I believe that would be the right thing to do, before I begin to preach to you, to help this poor man so that he shall enjoy the meeting like us, without any pain. (The man referred to was in pain with his head wrapped up in a bandage), and after he was prayed for he testified that he had absolutely no pain.

Smith - If you want to grow in God's grace; get hungry to be fed by it, thirsty to cry out for it & broken so you can't live without it.

Have Faith in God

#82   A man came to me in one of my meetings who had seen other people healed and wanted to be healed, too. He explained that his arm had been fixed in a certain position for many years and he could not move it. I said to him "Got any faith?". He said He had a lot of faith. After prayer he was able to swing his arm round and round. But he was not satisfied and complained, "I feel a little bit of trouble just there," pointing to a certain place. "Do you know what is the trouble with you I said to him?" He answered, "No." I said, "Imperfect faith." "What things so ever ye desire, when ye pray, believe that ye receive them and ye shall have them."

Smith - The Word of God is the food of faith.

#83 I realize that God can never bless us when we are hardhearted, critical or unforgiving. This will hinder faith quicker than anything in the world. I remember being at a meeting where there were some people waiting for God for the Baptism-seeking for cleansing, for the moment a person is cleansed the Spirit will fall. There was one man with eyes red from weeping bitterly. He said to me, "I shall have to leave. It is no good my staying without I change things. I have written a letter to my brother-in-law, and filled it with hard words, and this thing must first be taken care of" He went home and told his wife, "I'm going to write a letter to your brother and ask him to forgive me for writing to him the way I did." "You fool!" she said. "Never mind," he replied, "this is between God and me, and it has got to be dealt with." He wrote the letter and came again, and straightway God filled him with the Spirit.

I believe there are a great many people who would be healed, but they are harboring things in their hearts that is grieving the Holy Spirit. Let these things be dealt with in your heart. Forgive, and the Lord will forgive you. There are many good people, people that mean well, but they have no power to do anything for God. There is just some little thing that came in their hearts years ago, and their faith has been paralyzed ever since. Bring everything to the light. God will wash it all away with his blood if you will let Him. Let the precious blood of Christ cleanse you from all sin. If you will but believe, God will meet you and bring into your lives the sunshine of His love.

Smith - "One half of the trouble in the assemblies is the people's murmuring over the conditions they are in. The Bible teaches us not to murmur. If you reach that standard, you will never murmur anymore. You will be above murmuring. You will be in the place where God is absolutely the exchanger of thought, the exchanger of actions, and the exchanger of your inward purity. He will be purifying you all the time and lifting you higher, and you will know you are not of this world (John 15:19)."

From: Pentecostal Evangel.

#84   Mrs. E. Curtis of Christchurch, New Zealand, was suffering with septic poisoning in the blood. She had become only a skeleton and the doctors could do nothing for her. She had agonizing pains all day and all night. She was healed immediately when prayer was made for her in the name of Jesus. She states that for the past sixteen years she has been afflicted by severe pain but is now wonderfully well. Another testified to healing of deafness, goiter, adenoids and bad eyesight. Another testified to healing of double curvature of the spine from infancy, hip disease, weak heart, leg lengthened three inches, which grew normal like the other leg. It was also three inches less in circumference. She wore a large boot but now walks on even feet, the large boot having been discarded. Another was healed from a goiter through a handkerchief that had been prayed on.

Smith - "There is a place where God, through the power of the Holy Ghost, reigns supreme in our lives."

Sermon: Himself Took Our Infirmities

#85   A woman came to me in the city of Liverpool and said, "I would like you to help me. I wish you would join with me in prayer. My husband is a drunkard and every night comes into the home under the influence of drink. Won't you join me in prayer for him?" I said to the woman, "Have you a handkerchief?" She took out a handkerchief and I prayed over it and told her to lay it on the pillow of the drunken man. Her husband came home that night and laid his head on the pillow in which this handkerchief was tucked. He laid his head on more than the pillow that night. He laid his head on the promise of God. In Mark 11 :24, we read, "What things so ever ye desire when ye pray, believe that ye receive them and ye shall have them."

The next morning the man got up and called at the first saloon that he had to pass on his way to work and ordered some beer. He tasted it and said to the bartender, "You have poisonend this beer." He could not drink it, and went on to the next saloon and ordered some more beer. He tasted it and said to the man behind the counter, "You put poison in this beer, I believe you folks have agreed to poison me." The bartender was indignant at being thus charged. The man said, "I will go somewhere else." He went to another saloon and the same thing happened as in the two previous saloons. He made such a fuss that they threw him out. After he came out from work he went to another saloon to get some beer, and again he thought he had been poisoned and he made so much disturbance that he was thrown out there to. He went to his home and told his wife what had happened and said, ".It seems as though all the fellows have agreed to poison me." His wife said to him, "Can't you see the hand of the Lord in this, that He is making you dislike the stuff that has been your destruction?" This word brought conviction to the man's heart and he came to the meeting and got saved. The Lord has still power to set the captives free.

Smith - "Before a man can bind the enemy, he must know there is nothing binding him."

#86   When I was in Australia a lady came to me who was much troubled about her son who was so lazy and refused to work. I prayed over a handkerchief which I had her place on the boy's pillow. He slept that night on the handkerchief and the next morning he jumped up out of bed and went out and secured a position and went to work. Oh, praise the Lord, you can't shut God out, but if you will only believe He will shut the devil out.

Smith - "Inactivity is a robber which steals blessings. Increase comes by action, by using what we have and know...going on from faith to faith."

#87   When I was in Australia a man came up to me. He was leaning on a big stick and said, "I would like you to help me. It will take you about an half an hour to pray for me." I said, "Believe God and in one moment you will be whole." His faith was quickened to receive an immediate healing and he went away glorifying God for a miraculous healing. The word of the Lord is sufficient today. If you will dare to believe God's Word you will see a performance of His Word that will be truly wonderful.

Smith - "I want to help you decide that by the power of God, you will not be ordinary!"

#88   I received a telegram once urging me to visit a case about 200 miles from my home. As I went to this place I met the father and mother and found them broken hearted. They lead me up a staircase to a room and I saw a young woman on the floor and five people were holding her down. She was a frail young woman but the demonic power in her was greater than all those young men. As I went into the room the evil powers looked out of her eyes and they used her lips saying, "We are many, you can't cast us out." I said, "**Jesus can.**" He is more than enough in every situation. He is waiting for an opportunity to bless, heal and deliver. He is ready to save and to deliver souls. When we receive Jesus it becomes a reality in us that, **"Greater is He that is in you than he that is in the world."** He is greater than all the powers of darkness. No man can meet the devil in his own strength, but any man filled with the knowledge of Jesus, filled with His presence, filled with His power, filled with faith is more than a match for the powers of darkness. God has called us to be more than conquerors through Him that loved us.

The living Word is able to destroy Satanic forces. There is power in the name of Jesus. I would that every window in the street had the name of Jesus written large upon it. His name, through faith in His name. brought deliverance to this poor, bound soul, and thirty-seven demons came out giving their names as they came forth. The dear woman was completely delivered and they were able to give her back her child. That night there was heaven in that home and the father and mother, son and his wife were all united in glorifying Christ for His infinite grace. The next morning we had a gracious time in the breaking of bread. All things are wonderful with our wonderful Jesus. If you would dare rest your all upon Him, things would take place and He would change your whole circumstance. In a moment, through the name of Jesus, a new life can be realized.

Smith - "A man must be in an immoveable condition. The voice of God must mean more to him than what he sees, feels or what people say"

#89   One year ago my husband was instantly healed of double rupture of 3 years' standing, dropsy (2 years), a weak heart, and tobacco chewing (47 years), and praise the Lord, it was all taken away when the power of heaven went straight through him. Nine weeks ago today we went to Portland, Oregon, to hear Brother Smith Wigglesworth, and my husband was healed instantly of heavy blood-pressure and varicose veins which had broken in his ankles and for a year had to be dressed twice a day. No doctor could help him, but, praise God, Jesus was the doctor and healed him. Should anyone wish to write me, I shall be glad to hear from them and will answer all letters.-Mrs. Frank Nephews, 202 E. 1st St., Newberg, Ore.

Smith - Lord, give us, Thy servants, great searching's of heart, great decisions of will and great assurances through the blood of Jesus.

Sermon: I Am the Lord That

#90   One day I had been visiting the sick, and was with a friend of mine, an architect, when I saw a young man from his office coming down the road in a car, and holding in his hand a telegram. It contained a very urgent request that we go immediately to pray for a man who was dying. We went off in an auto as fast as possible and in about an hour and a half reached a large house in the country where the man who was dying resided.

There were two staircases in that house, and it was extremely convenient, for the doctors could go up and down one, and my friend and I could go up and down the other, and so we had no occasion to meet.

I found on arrival that had been physically hurt. The man's body had been broken, he was ruptured, and his bowels had been punctured in two places. The discharge from the bowels had formed abscesses, and blood poisoning had set in. The man's face had turned green. Two doctors were in attendance, but they saw that the case was beyond their power. They had telegraphed to London for a great specialist, and, when we arrived, they were at the railway station awaiting for this physician's arrival.

The man was very near death when we arrived and could not speak. I said to his wife, "If you desire, we will anoint and pray for him in the name of Jesus." She said, "That is why I sent for you." I anointed him in the name of the Lord and asked the Lord to raise him up. At that moment there was no change. (God often hides what He does. From day to day we find that God is doing wonderful things, and we receive reports of healings that have taken place that we heard nothing about at the time of our meetings. Only last night a woman came into the meeting suffering terribly. Her whole arm was filled with poison, and her blood was so poisoned that it was certain to bring her to her death. We rebuked the thing, and she was here this morning and told us that she was without pain and had slept all night, a thing she had not done for two months. To God be all the praise. You will find He will do this kind of thing all the time.)

As soon as we anointed and prayed for this brother we went down the back staircase and the three doctors came up the front staircase. As we arrived downstairs, I said to my friend who had come with me, "Friend let me have hold of your hands." We held each other's hands, and I said to him, "Look to God and let us agree together, according to Matthew 18:19, that this man shall be brought out of this death." We took the whole situation before God, and said, "Father, we believe."

Then the conflict began. The wife came down to us and said, "The doctors have got all their instruments out and they are about to operate on him." I cried, "**What**? Look here, he's your husband, and I tell you this, if those men operate on him, he will die. Go back and tell them you cannot allow it." She went back to the doctors and said, "Give me ten minutes." They said, "We can't afford to, the man is dying and it is your husband's only chance." She said, "I want ten minutes, and you don't touch him until I have those 10 minutes."

They went downstairs by one staircase and we went up by the other. I said to the woman, "This man is your husband, and he cannot speak for himself. It is now the time for you to put your whole trust in God and prove Him wholly true. You can save him from a thousand doctors. You must stand with God and for God in this critical hour." After that, we came down and the doctors went up. The wife faced those three doctors and said, "You will not touch my man's body. He is my husband. I am sure that if you operate on him he will die, but he will live if you don't touch him."

Suddenly the man in the bed spoke. "God has done it," he said. They rolled back the bed clothes and the doctors examined him, and the abscesses were cut clear away. The nurse cleaned the place where they had been. The doctors could see the bowels still open and they said to the wife, "We know that you have great faith, and we can see that a miracle has taken place. But you must let us unite these broken parts and put in silver tubes, and we know that your husband will be all right after that, and it need not interfere with your faith at all." She said to them, "God has done the first thing and He can do the rest. No man shall touch him now." And God healed the whole thing. That same man is well and strong today. I can give his name and address to any who want it.

Smith - I do not ask my body how it feels. I TELL my body how it feels!

#91　　My boys did not know anything else but to trust the Lord as the family Physician, and my youngest boy, George, cried out from the attic, "Dadda, come." I cried, "I cannot come. The whole thing is because of me. I shall have to repent and ask the Lord to forgive me." I made up my mind to humble myself before the whole church. Then I rushed to the attic and laid my hands on my boy in the name of Jesus. I placed my hands on his head and the pain left and went lower down; he cried again, "Put your hands still lower." At last the pain went right down to the feet and as I placed my hand on the feet be was completely delivered. Some evil power had evidently gotten a hold of him and as I laid my hands on the different parts of the body it left. (We have to see the difference between anointing the sick and casting out demons.) God will always be gracious when we humble ourselves before Him and come to a place of brokenness of spirit.

Smith - No wavering! A definite faith brings a definite experience and a definite utterance.

#92　　I was at a place one time ministering to a sick woman, and she said, "I'm very sick. I become all right for an hour, and then I have another attack." I saw that it was an evil power that was attacking her, and I learned something in that hour that I had never learned before. As I moved my hand down her body in the name of the Lord that evil power seemed to move just ahead of my hands and as I moved them down further and further the evil power went right out of her body and never returned.

Smith - I am never at my best until I am in a conflict - until I have a fight with the enemy!

#93   I was in Havre in France and the power of God was being mightily manifested. A Greek named Felix attended the meeting and became very zealous for God. He was very anxious to get all the Catholics he could to the meeting in order that they should see that God was graciously visiting France. He found a certain bed-ridden woman who was fixed in a certain position and could not move, and he told her about the Lord healing at the meetings and that he would get me to come if she wished. She said, "My husband is a Catholic and he would never allow anyone who was not a Catholic to see me."

She asked her husband to allow me to come and told him what Felix had told her about the power of God working in our midst. He said, "I will have no Protestant enter my house." She said, "You know the doctors cannot help me, and the priests cannot help, won't you let this man of God pray for me?" He finally consented and I went to the house. The simplicity of this woman and her child-like faith were beautiful to see.

I showed her my oil bottle and said to her, "Here is oil. It is a symbol of the Holy Ghost. When that comes upon you, the Holy Ghost will begin to work, and the Lord will raise you up." And God did something the moment the oil fell upon her. I looked toward the window and I saw Jesus. (I have seen Him often. There is no painting that is anywhere near like Him, no artist can ever depict the beauty of my lovely Lord.) The woman felt the power of God in her body and cried, "I'm free, my hands are free, my shoulders are free, and oh, I see Jesus! I'm free! I'm free!"

The vision vanished and the woman sat up in bed. Her legs were still bound, and I said to her, "I'll put my hands over your legs and you will be free entirely." And as I put my hands on those legs (they were covered with bed clothes), I looked and saw the Lord again. She saw Him too and cried, "He's there again. I'm free! I'm free!" She rose from her bed and walked round the room praising God, and we were all in tears as we saw His wonderful works. The Lord shall raise them up when all the right conditions are met.

Smith - There is healing through the blood of Christ and deliverance for every captive.

#94   I was one time asked to go to Weston-super-mare, a seaside resort in the West of England. I learned from a telegram that a man had lost his reason and had become a raving maniac, and they wanted me to go to pray for him. I arrived at the place, and the wife said to me, "Will you stay overnight while my husband sleeps?" I agreed, and in the middle of the night an evil power laid hold of him. It was awful. I put my hand on his head and his hair stuck straight up like they were a lot of sticks. God gave deliverance-a temporary deliverance at that time. At 6 o'clock the next morning, I felt that it was necessary that I should get out of the house for a short time.

The man saw me going and cried out, "If you leave me, there is no hope." But I felt that I had to go, telling him I will be back in a little. As I went out I saw a woman with a Salvation Army bonnet on and I knew that she was going to their 7 o'clock prayer meeting. I said to the Captain who was in charge of the meeting, when I saw he was about to give out a hymn, "Captain, please don't sing. Could we go to prayer right away? He agreed, and I prayed my heart out to the Lord, and then the spirit moves me and I grabbed my hat and rushed out of the hall. They all thought they had a madman in their prayer meeting that morning.

I saw the man I had spent the night with, he was rushing down toward the sea, without a particle of clothing on, about to drown himself. I cried, "In the name of Jesus, come out of him!" At that moment the man fell full length on the ground and that evil power went out of him never to return. His wife came rushing after him, and the husband was restored to her in a perfect mental condition.

Smith - It is an insult to ask God for power after you have received the baptism of the Holy Ghost. You have power! You have to act!

TEACHING FROM SMITH WIGGLESWORTH

* HIS ATTITUDE TOWARDS CALVINISM

God says to us, "In patience possess thy soul." How beautiful! There have been in England great churches which believed once saved always saved. I thank God that they are all disappearing. You will find if you go to England those hardheaded people that used to hold on to these things are almost gone. Why? Because they went on to say whatever you did, if you were elect, you were right. That is so wrong.

The elect of God are those that keep pressing forward. The elect of God cannot hold still. They are always on the move. Every person that has a knowledge of the elect of God realizes it is important that he continues to press forward. He cannot endure sin nor darkness's nor things done in the shadows. The elect is so in earnest to be right for God that he burns every bridge behind him.

"Knowing this, that first there shall be a falling away"

Knowing this, that first God shall bring into His treasury the realities of the truth and put them side by side — the false, and the true, those that can be shaken in mind, and those that cannot be shaken in mind. God requires us to be so built upon the foundation of truth that we cannot be shaken in our mind, it doesn't matter what comes.

* IN THE NEW COVENANT THE 10 COMMANDMENTS ARE DONE AWAY WITH!

"Done away! Done away!" Henceforth there is a new cry in our hearts, "I delight to do Thy will, O God." He taketh away the first, the ministration of death, written and engrave in stones, that He might establish the second, this ministration of righteousness, this life in the Spirit. You ask, "Does a man who is filled with the Spirit cease to keep the commandments?" I simply repeat what the Spirit of God has told us here, that this ministration of death, written and engrave in stones (and you know that the ten commandments were written on stones) is "DONE AWAY." The man who becomes a living epistle of Christ, written with the Spirit of the living God, has ceased to be an adulterer, or a murderer or a covetous man; the will of God is his delight. I love to do the will of God; there is no irksomeness to it; it is no trial to pray; no trouble to read the Word of God; it is not a hard thing to go to the place of worship. With the psalmist you say, "I was glad when they said unto me, Let us go into the house of the Lord."

How does this new life work out? The thing works out because God works in you to will and to do of His own good pleasure (Phil. 2:13). There is a great difference between a pump and a spring. The law is a pump, the Baptism is a spring. The old pump gets out of order, the parts perish, and the well runs dry. The letter killeth. But the spring is ever bubbling up and there is a ceaseless flow direct from the throne of God. There is life.

It is written of Christ, "Thou lovest righteousness, and hatest wickedness." And in this new life in the Spirit, in this new covenant life, you love the things that are right and pure and holy, and shudder at all things that are wrong. Jesus was able to say, "The prince of this world cometh, and bath nothing in Me," and the moment we are filled with the Spirit of God we are brought into like wonderful condition, and, as we continue to be filled with the Spirit, the enemy cannot have an inch of territory in us.

EXPERIENCES FROM THE AUTHOR

How God Gave Me Victory over Painful Tumors

I woke up one morning with tremendous pain in my lower abdomen. I lifted up my shirt and looked down where the pain was. There was a very hard lump on my abdomen about the size of an acorn. I laid my hands on it immediately, commanding it to go. I said "You lying devil, by the stripes of Jesus I am healed and made whole." After I spoke to the lump, the pain became excruciating and overwhelmingly worse. All that day I walked the floor crying out to God, and praising him that His Word is real and true. I went for a walk on the mountain right behind the parsonage.

It was a long day before I got to sleep that night. When I awoke the next morning the pain was even more severe. It felt like somebody was stabbing me in my gut with a knife and twisting it.

I lifted up my shirt and looked and there was another hard lump. Now I had two lumps in my lower abdomen. I laid my hands on them, commanding them to go. Tears were rolling down my face, as I spoke the Word of God. I lifted my hands toward heaven and kept praising God that I was healed. Even though I did not see any change, I kept praising God. All the symptoms were telling me that God's Word is a lie, and that I was not healed by the stripes of Jesus. But I knew that I was healed. It was another long day. It seemed as if I could never get to sleep that night. The pain was continual and non-stop!

When I got up the next morning the pain had intensified even more. Once again I looked at my abdomen and to my shock and torment there was another lump the size of an acorn. Now I had three of these nasty very hard lumps and each were about the size of an acorn. I did not think that the pain could get any worse, but it was. Once again I laid my hands on these tumors, commanding them to go in the name of Jesus Christ of Nazareth. I declared that by the stripes of Jesus I am healed! It felt like a knife sticking in my gut all that day and night.

I lifted my hands, and with tears rolling down my face. I kept praising God that I was healed. By faith I began to dance before the Lord a victory dance, praising God that I was healed by the stripes of Jesus. My wife saw me as I had my hands lifted up praising God and dancing before the Lord. I knew, that I knew, that I knew that God cannot lie. That I was healed by His stripes. Those lumps could not stay on my body in the name of Jesus.

I went to bed that night hurting worse than ever. All night I tossed, turned, and moaned, all the while thanking God that I was not going to die but that I was healed. I got up the next morning, and all of the tumors and pain were completely gone. They have never come back.

CHAPTER SIX

Sermon: Immersed in the Holy Ghost

#95   The last three months have been the greatest days of my life. I used to think if I could see such and such things happening I should be satisfied; but I have seen greater things than I ever expected to see, and I am now more hungry to see greater things yet. The great thing at conventions is to get us so immersed in God that we may see him manifest himself in signs and wonders in the name of the Lord Jesus; a place where death has taken place and we are not our own any longer, for God has taken us. If God has taken hold of us we will be changed by His power and might. You can depend on it, the Ethiopian will be changed. I find God has a plan to turn the world upside down, and to take us to places we have not yet been.

Smith - "I do not ever ask Smith Wigglesworth how he feels!" I simply jump out of bed every morning! I dance before the Lord for at least 10 to 12 minutes – high speed dancing. I jump up and down and run around my room telling God how great he is, how wonderful He is, how glad I am to be associated with Him and to be His child."

#96   If I am filled with the Holy Ghost, He will formulate the word that will come into my heart. The sound of my voice is only by the breath that goes through it. When I was in a little room at Bern waiting for my passport, I found a lot of people, but I couldn't speak to them. So I got hold of three men and pulled them unto me. They stared, but I got them on their knees. Then we prayed, and the revival began. I couldn't talk to them, but I could show them the way to talk to Someone else.

God will move upon the people to make them see the glory of God just as it was when Jesus walked in this world, and I believe the Holy Ghost will do special wonders and miracles in these last days. I was taken to see a young woman who was very ill. The young man who showed me the way said, "I am afraid we shall not be able to do much here, because of her mother, and the doctors are coming." I said, "This is what God has brought me here for," and when I prayed the young woman was instantly healed by the power of God. God the Holy Ghost says in our hearts today that it is only He who can do it. After that we got crowds, and I ministered to the sick among them for two hours.

Smith - Being hardhearted, critical or unforgiving will hinder faith quicker than anything.

Sermon: Life in the Spirit

#97 I don't want to boast. If I glory in anything, it is only in the Lord who has been so gracious to me. But I remember one time stepping out of a railroad carriage to wash my hands. I had a season of prayer, and the Lord just filled me to overflowing with His love. I was going to a convention in Ireland, and I could not get there fast enough. As I returned, I believe that the Spirit of the Lord was so heavily upon me that my face must have shone. (No man can tell himself when the Spirit transforms his very countenance.) There were two clerical mere sitting together, and as I got into the carriage again, one of them cried out, "You convince me of sin." Within three minutes every one in the carriage was crying to God for salvation. This thing has happened many times in my life. It is this ministration of the Spirit that Paul speaks of, this filling of the Spirit, that will make your life effective, so that even the people in the stores where you trade will want to leave your presence because they are brought under conviction.

Smith - All lack of faith is due to not feeding on God's Word. You need it every day

Sermon: Paul's vision and the baptism of the Holy Ghost.

#98   There was a dear woman, her heart was in a bad way, poor soul, her feet were swelled. When the devil gets your eyes he makes you look at death. I said, "I believe the Lord wants you to have His life saving message." I saw she saw death. It is a tremendous power Satan has when we have taken our eyes off Jesus, but He is alive, and He is risen to make everything living, and His glory is life for evermore. I thought I would show this dear woman that He has the keys and she might take the promise for a new heart (Psalm 91) and "with long life will I satisfy him." "Oh," she said, "it is a new word to me." "Yes," I said, "all revelation is new." In 3 days God did wonders. She had risen right into the condition of this life. She said, "It is Amen, I have a new heart, my legs are not swelled." It is no good without it is the Amen from above. The Amen—what does it mean—"let it be." It was Jesus who said it—it was He who was Clothed who said it—The One from heaven, the One who had won the victory, and God wants us to do it in His place.

Smith - "The moment a man falls into sin, divine life ceases to flow, and his life becomes one of helplessness."

Sermon: On resurrection power

#99 Last week I went into a house where they were very much in great distress. A young woman was there who, they told me, had not been able to drink for six years. Her body had been rapidly degrading, but the Lord had inspired her with faith and she said to her father, "O Father, I ought to have relief to-day. Somehow I feel this whole trouble ought to go to-day." I knew what it was. It was a demon in the throat. I believe that the devil is at the bottom of practically every evil in human lives. It was a serious thing to see that beautiful young woman, who, because of this one thing in her life, was so disorganized in her mind and body. I knew it was the power of Satan. How did I know? Because it attacked her at a vital point, and the thing had preyed on her mind and she was filled with fear so that she said, "I dare not drink, for if I do I shall choke."

Deliverance to the captives. I asked the father and mother to go out of the room and then I said to the young woman, "You will be free and drink as much as you want when I have done with you if you will only believe. As sure as you are there you will drink as much as you want." I said further, "Our brethren are going out in the streets to preach to-night and I shall be among them, and in our preaching we will say definitely, 'Every one that will believe on the Lord Jesus Christ can be saved.' We will also tell them that everyone that believes can be healed. The Word of God shows us plainly that the Son of God bore our sins and our sicknesses at Calvary. They will emphasize it over and over again. It is just as true to say, 'Himself took our infirmities and bare our sicknesses,' as it is to say, 'He was wounded for our transgressions, He was bruised for our iniquities.' " So I said to her, "Now do you believe?" She said, "Yes, I believe that in the name of Jesus you can cast the evil power out." I then laid my hands on her in the name of Jesus. "It is done, you drink."

She went out laughingly and drew the first glass of water and drank. She cried out, "Mother! Father! Brother! I have drunk one glass!" There was joy in the house. What did it? It was the living faith of the Son of God. Oh, if we only knew how rich we are, and how near we are to the Fountain of life. "All things are possible to him that believeth."

Smith - "If the spirit does not move me, I move the Spirit."

Sermon: Precious Faith

#100   I remember in the year 1920 after a most distressing voyage I went straight from the ship on which I had been traveling to a meeting. As I entered the building a man fell down across the doorway in a seizure. The Spirit of the Lord was upon me and I commanded the demon to leave him immediately. Some years later I visited this same assembly, and I ventured to ask if anyone remembered the incident. A man stood up and I told him to come to the platform. He told me that on that day he had been delivered by the name of Jesus and had not had a seizure since.

Smith - "Because you are joint-heirs, you have a RIGHT to healing for your body & to be delivered from ALL the power of the enemy"

#101   I remember a man coming to me suffering with cancer, who said he had been twelve years in this terrible pain. The power of the Lord was present to heal the sick, and that night he came back to the meeting with all his sores dried up.

Smith - "When the Holy Spirit comes, He ALWAYS brings a rich revelation of Christ."

#102   When I was in Orebro 12 years ago I ministered to a girl who was twelve years' old, and blind. When I last went to Orebro they told me that she had had perfect sight from that day forward. The Lord Himself challenges us to believe Him when He says, "Have faith in God." "Verily, I say unto you, That whosoever shall say unto this mountain., Be thou removed, and be thou cast into the sea; and shall not doubt in his heart, but shall believe that those things which he saith shall come to pass; he shall have whatsoever he saith." Did you get that? "He shall have whatsoever he saith." When you speak in faith your desire is an accomplished reality. Our Lord further said, "Therefore I say unto you, What things soever ye desire, when ye pray, believe that ye receive them, and ye shall have them."

Smith - "No-one can live after seeing God; and God wants us ALL to see Him so that we shall joyfully cease to be--and that HE may become our life."

#103   In one place a man said to me, "You helped a good many today, but you have not helped me." I said, "What is the trouble?" He said, "I cannot sleep, and I am losing my mind." I said to him, "Believe." And then I told him to go home and sleep, and I told him I would believe God with him. He went home and his wife said to him, "Well, did you see the preacher?" And he said, "He helped everyone but me." However, he fell asleep when his head hit the pillow. His wife said, "I wonder if it is all right." Morning, noon, and night he was still asleep, but he woke up bright and happy, rested and restored. What had brought about this restoration? Faith in God! "He shall have whatsoever he saith."

Smith - "No man can save you. No man can heal you. If anyone has been healed in my meetings, it is the Lord that has healed them."

Sermon: Present-Time Blessings

#104   My wife once said to me, "You watch me when I'm preaching. Someday I will get so close to heaven that when I'm preaching I'll be off." One night she was preaching and when she had finished, off she went. I was going to Glasgow and had said goodbye to her before she went to the meeting that night. As I was leaving the house, the doctor and policeman met me at the door and told me that she had fallen dead at the Mission door. I knew she had got what she wanted. I could not weep, but I was in tongues, praising the Lord.

On the natural lines she was everything to me; but I could not mourn on natural lines, but just laughed in the Spirit. The house was soon filled with people. The doctor said, "She is dead, and we can do no more for her." I went up to her lifeless corpse and commanded death to give her up, and she came back to me for a moment. Then God said to me, "She is Mine; her work is done." I knew what He meant.

They laid her in the coffin, and I brought my sons and my daughter into the room and said, "Is she there?" They said, "No, father." I said, "We will cover her body up." If you go mourning the loss of loved ones who have gone to be with Christ, I say it in love to you, you have never had the revelation of what Paul spoke of when he showed us that it is better to go than to stay. We read this in Scripture, but the trouble is that people will not believe it. When you believe God, you will say, "Whatever it is, it is all right. If You want to take the one I love, it is all right, Lord." Faith removes all tears of self-pity.

Smith - 'To bring deliverance for the captives!' This is why the Lord baptizes us in the Holy Ghost!

#105   In our Sunday school we had a boy with red hair. His head was as red as fire and so was his temper. He was such a trial. He kicked his teachers and the superintendent. He was simply uncontrollable. The teachers had a meeting in which they discussed the matter of expelling him. They thought that God might undertake for that boy and so they decided to give him another chance. One day he had to be turned away, and he broke all the windows of the mission. He was worse outside than in.

Sometime later we had a ten-days revival meeting. There was nothing much doing in that meeting and people thought it a waste of time, but there was one result--the redheaded lad got saved. After he was saved, the difficulty was to get rid of him at our house. He would be there until midnight crying to God to make him pliable and use him for His glory. God delivered the lad from his temper and made him one of the meekest, most beautiful boys you ever saw. For twenty years he has been a mighty missionary in China. God takes us just as we are and transforms us by His power.

Smith - The Lord has called us into heart union with Himself. He wants His bride to have one heart and one Spirit with Himself.

#106   I can remember the time when I used to go white with rage, and shake all over with temper. I could hardly hold myself together. I waited on God for ten days. In those ten days I was being emptied out and the life of the Lord Jesus was being wrought into me. My wife testified of the transformation that took place in my life, "I never saw such a change. I have never been able to cook anything since that time that has not pleased him. Nothing is too hot or too cold, everything is just right." God must come and reign supreme in your life. Will you let Him do it? He can do it, and He will if you will let Him. It is no use trying to tame the "old man." But God can deal with him. The carnal mind will never be subjected to God, but God will bring it to the cross where it belongs, and will put in its place, the pure, the holy, the meek mind of the Master.

Smith - When the Word and the Spirit come together, there will be the biggest move of the Holy Spirit that the world has ever seen.

#107   In Switzerland, I learned of a man who met with the assembly of the Plymouth Brethren. He attended their various meetings, and one morning, at their breaking of bread service, he arose and said, "Brethren, we have the Word, and I feel that we are living very much in the letter of it, but there is a hunger and thirst in my soul for something deeper, something more real than we have, and I cannot rest until I enter into it." The next Sunday this brother rose again and said, "We are all so poor here, there is no life in this assembly, and my heart is hungry for reality." He did this for several weeks until it got on the nerves of those people and they protested. "Sands, you are making us all miserable. You are spoiling our meetings, and there is only one thing for you to do, and that is to clear out."

That man went out of the meeting in a very sad condition. As he stood outside, one of his children asked him what was the matter, and he said, "To think that they should turn me out from their midst for being hungry and thirsty for more of God!" I did not know anything of this until afterward.

Some days later someone rushed up to Sands and said, "There is a man over here from England, and he is speaking about tongues and healing." Sands said, "I'll fix him. I'll go to the meeting and sit right up in the front and challenge him with the Scriptures. I'll dare him to preach these things in Switzerland. I'll publicly denounce him." So he came to the meetings. There he sat. He was so hungry and thirsty that he drank in every word that was said. His opposition soon died out. The first morning he said to a friend, "This is what I want." He drank and drank of the Spirit. After three weeks he said, "God will have to do something now or I'll burst." He breathed in God and the Lord filled him to such an extent that he spoke in other tongues as the Spirit gave utterance. Sands is now preaching, and is in charge of a new Pentecostal assembly.

Smith - Feed on the living Christ and the faith of God will spring up within you!

Sermon: Resurrection Life

#108   While ministering in one place, we had a banquet for people who were diseased--people who were lame and weary, blind and sick in every way. A dear man got hold of a boy who was encased in iron from top to bottom, lifted him up, and placed him onto the platform. Hands were laid on him in the name of Jesus.

"Papa! Papa! Papa!" the boy said. "It's going all over me! Oh, Papa, come and take these irons off!" I do like to hear children speak; they say such wonderful things. The father took the irons off, and the life of God had gone all over the boy!

Don't you know this is the resurrection touch? This is the divine life; this is what God has brought us into. Let it go over us, Lord-- the power of the Holy Spirit, the resurrection of heaven, the sweetness of Your blessing, the joy of the Lord!

Smith - Enter into the promises of God. It is your inheritance.

Sermon: Righteousness

#109   One day I was having a meeting in Bury, in Lancashire, England. A young woman was present who came from a place called Rams bottom, to be healed of a goiter. Before she came she said, "I am going to be healed of this goiter, mother." After one meeting she came forward and was prayed for. The next meeting she got up and testified that she had been wonderfully healed, and she said, "I shall be so happy to go and tell mother that I have been wonderfully healed." She went to her home and testified how wonderfully she had been healed, and the next year when we were having the convention she came again. To the natural view it looked as though the goiter was just as big as ever; but that young woman was believing God and she was soon on her feet giving her testimony, and saying, "I was here last year and the Lord wonderfully healed me. I want to tell you that this has been the best year of my life." She seemed to be greatly blessed in that meeting and she went home to testify more strongly than ever that the Lord had healed her. She believed God. The third year she was at the meeting again, and some people who looked at her said, "How big that goiter has become." But when the time came for testimony she was up on her feet and testified, "Two years ago the Lord graciously healed me of goiter. Oh I had a most wonderful healing. It is grand to be healed by the power of God."

That day someone remonstrated with her and said, "People will think there is something the matter with you. Why don't you look in the glass? You will see your goiter is bigger than ever." That good woman went to the Lord about it and said, "Lord, you so wonderfully healed me two years ago. Won't you show all the people that you healed me." She went to sleep peacefully that night still believing God and when she came down the next day there was not a trace or a mark of that goiter.

Smith - Now listen! God's plan for you is to forget the past because the future is so amazingly wonderful!

#110   One day I was preaching and a man brought a boy who was all wrapped up in bandages. The boy was in irons and it was impossible for him to walk and it was difficult for them to get him to the platform. They passed him over about six seats. The power of the Lord was present to heal the sick and it entered right into the child as I placed my hands on him. The child cried, "Daddy, it is going all over me." They stripped the boy and found nothing imperfect in him.

Smith - What is faith? It is the very nature of God. Faith is the Word of God...the personal inward flow of divine favour,

Sermon: Sons of God—now!

#111   I have lived in one house for sixty years. I have preached from my own doorstep, and all the people in our neighborhood know me. They know me when they need someone to pray for them, when they are in trouble, or when they are in any special need. But when they call their friends, do they call me? No! Why? They would say, "He is sure to want a prayer meeting, but we want to dance." Wherever Jesus came, sin was revealed, and men did not like sin revealed. But it is sin that separates us from God forever.

You are in a good place when you become sensitive to the least sin and weep before God about it, repenting over the least thing in which you have grieved Him. You may have spoken unkindly; you realize that it was not like the Lord, and your conscience has taken you to prayer. It is a wonderful thing to have a sensitive conscience. It is when we are close to God that our hearts are revealed to us; it is then we learn to loathe ourselves, and the Holy Spirit turns us to Christ. We take Him to be our righteousness and our holiness. God intends us to live in purity. He has said, "Blessed are the pure in heart: for they shall see God." And the pure in heart can see Him all the time in everything.

Smith - The moment a man falls into sin, divine life ceases to flow, and his life becomes one of helplessness

#112　　One time, on board ship, a young man came to me and asked me to take part in a sweepstake. I said to him, "I am preaching on Sunday. Will you come if I do?" He said, "No!" Later there was onboard entertainment. I said I would like to take part. It was the strangest thing for me. I said I would sing. I saw men dressed as clergymen entertaining the people with foolishness. I was troubled. I cried out to God. Then came my turn, just before the dance. A young woman came to take my book and accompany me. She was only half dressed. She said, "I can't play that!" I said, "Never worry." Then I sang, *"If I could only tell you how I love Him, I am sure that you would make Him yours today!"* There was no dance. A number began to weep, and six young men gave their hearts to God in my cabin.

No man that sins has power. Sin makes a man weak. Sin dethrones, but purity strengthens. Temptation is not sin. The devil is a liar, and he will try to take away your peace. But we must always live in the Word of God and on that scripture which tells us, "There is therefore now no condemnation to them that are in Christ Jesus." If Christ condemns you not, who is he that can condemn you? Do not condemn yourself. If there is anything wrong, confess it out and then come to the blood of Jesus Christ. "If we confess our sins, He is faithful and just to forgive us our sins, and to cleanse us from all unrighteousness. If we walk in the light, as He is in the light, we have fellowship one with another, and the blood of Jesus Christ His Son cleanseth us from all sin."

Smith - I've never read a book but my Bible. Better to get the Book of books as food for the soul, strengthening of faith and building of character.

#113   Not long ago I received a wire asking me if I would go to Liverpool. There was a woman with cancer and gallstones, and she was very much discouraged. If I know God is sending me, my faith rises. The woman said, "I have no hope." I said, "Well, I have not come from Bradford to go home with a bad report." God said to me, "Establish her in the fact of the new birth." When she had the assurance that her sin was gone and she was born again, she said, "That's everything to me. The cancer is nothing now. I have got Jesus." The battle was won. God delivered her from her sin, from her sickness, and she was free, up and dressed, and happy in Jesus. When God speaks, it is as a nail in a sure place.

Will you believe, and will you receive Him? Life and immortality is ours in the gospel. This is our inheritance through the blood of Jesus—life for evermore!

Smith - In every weakness, God will be your strength. All you need is His touch.

Sermon: The Bible Evidence of the Baptism of the Spirit

#114   You know, beloved, it had to be something on the line of solid facts to move me. I was as certain as possible that I had received the Holy Ghost, and was absolutely rigid in this conviction. When this Pentecostal outpouring began in England I went to Sunderland and met with the people who had assembled for the purpose of receiving the Holy Ghost. I was continually in those meetings causing disturbances until the people wished I had never come. They said that I was disturbing the whole conditions. But I was hungry and thirsty for God, and had gone to Sunderland because I heard that God was pouring out His Spirit in a new way. I heard that God had now visited His people, had manifested His power and that people were speaking in tongues as on the day of Pentecost.

When I got to this place I said, "I cannot understand this meeting. I have left a meeting in Bradford all on fire for God. The fire fell last night and we were all laid out under the power of God. I have come here for tongues, and I don't hear them-I don't hear anything."

"Oh!" they said, "when you get baptized with the Holy Ghost you will speak in tongues." "Oh, is that it?" said I, "when the presence of God came upon me, my tongue was loosened, and really I felt as I went in the open air to preach that I had a new tongue." "Ah no," they said, "that is not it." "What is it, then?" I asked. They said, "When you get baptized in the Holy Ghost-" "I am baptized," I interjected, "and there is no one here who can persuade me that I am not baptized." So I was up against them arid they were up against me.

I remember a man getting up and saying, "You know, brothers and sisters, I was here three weeks and then the Lord baptized me with the Holy Ghost and I began to speak with other tongues." I said, "Let us hear it. That's what I'm here for." But he would not talk in tongues. I was doing what others are doing today, confusing the 12th of I Corinthians with the 2nd of Acts. These two chapters deal with different things, one with the gifts of the Spirit, and the other with the Baptism of the Spirit with the accompanying sign. I did not understand this and so I said to the man, "Let's hear you speak in tongues." But he could not. He had not received the "gift" of tongues, but the Baptism.

As the days passed I became more and more hungry. I had opposed the meetings so much, but the Lord was gracious, and I shall ever remember that last day-the day I was to leave. God was with me so much that last night. They were to have a meeting and I went, but I could not rest. I went to the Vicarage, and there in the library I said to Mrs. Boddy, "I cannot rest any longer, I must have these tongues." She replied, "Brother Wigglesworth, it is not the tongues you need but the Baptism. If you will allow God to baptize you, the other will be all right." "My dear sister, I know I am baptized," I said. "You know that I have to leave here at 4 o'clock. Please lay hands on me that I may receive the tongues."

She rose up and laid her hands on me and the fire fell. I said, "The fire's falling." Then came a persistent knock at the door, and she had to go out. That was the best thing that could have happened, for I was ALONE WITH GOD. Then He gave me a revelation. Oh, it was wonderful! He showed me an empty cross and Jesus glorified. I do thank God that the cross is empty, that Christ is no more on the cross. It was there that He bore the curse, for it is written, "Cursed is everyone that hangeth on a tree." He became sin for us that we might be made the righteousness of God in Him, and now, there He is in the glory. Then I saw that God had purified me. It seemed that God gave me a new vision, and I saw a perfect being within me with mouth open, saying, "Clean 1 Clean! Clean!" When I began to repeat it I found myself speaking in other tongues. The joy was so great that when I came to utter it my tongue failed, and I began to worship God in other tongues as the Spirit gave me utterance.

It was all as beautiful and peaceful as when Jesus said, "Peace, be still!" and the tranquility of that moment and the joy surpassed anything I had ever known up to that moment. But, Hallelujah 1 these days have grown with greater, mightier, more wonderful divine manifestations and power. That was but the beginning. There is no end to this kind of beginning. You will never get an end to the Holy Ghost till you are landed in the glory-till you are right in the presence of God forever. And even then we shall ever be conscious of His presence.

Smith - "It is a wonderful thing to pray in the Spirit and to sing in the Spirit, praying in tongues and singing in tongues as the Spirit of God gives you utterance."

TEACHING FROM SMITH WIGGLESWORTH

YOU DO NOT NEED drugs, quacks, pills and plasters

We have a big God. We have a wonderful Jesus. We have a glorious Comforter. God's canopy is over you and will cover you at all times, preserving you from evil. Under His wings shalt thou trust. The Word of God is living and powerful and in its treasures you will find eternal life. If you dare trust this wonderful Lord, this Lord of life, you will find in Him everything you need.

So many are tampering with drugs, quacks, pills and plasters. Clear them all out and believe God. It is sufficient to believe God. You will find that if you dare trust Him, He will never fail. "The prayer of faith shall save the sick, and the LORD shall raise him up." Do you trust Him? He is worthy to be trusted.

THE FRUIT OF THE SPIRIT!

There is a fruit of the Spirit that must accompany the gift of healing and that is longsuffering. The man who is going through with God to be used in healing must be a man of longsuffering. He must be always ready with a word of comfort. If the sick one is in distress and helpless and does not see everything eye to eye with you, you must bear with him. Our Lord Tesus Christ was filled with compassion and lived and moved in a place of longsuffering, and we will have to get into this place if we are to help needy ones.

There are some times when you pray for the sick and you are apparently rough. But you are not dealing with a person, you are dealing with the Satanic forces that are binding the person. Your heart is full of love and compassion to all, but you are moved to a holy anger as you see the place the devil has taken in the body of the sick one, and you deal with his position with a real forcefulness. One day a pet dog followed a lady out of her house and ran all round her feet. She said to the dog, "My dear, I cannot have you with me today." The dog wagged its tail and made a big fuss. She said, "Go home, my dear." But the dog did not go. At last she shouted roughly, "Go home," and off it went. Some people deal with the devil like that, The devil can stand all the comfort you like to give him. Cast him out! You are dealing not with the person, you are dealing with the devil. Demon power must be dislodged in the name of the Lord. You are always right when you dare to deal with sickness as with the devil. Much sickness is caused by some misconduct, there is something wrong, there is some neglect somewhere, and Satan has had a chance to get in. It is necessary to repent and confess where you have given place to the devil, and then he can be dealt with.

EXPERIENCES FROM THE AUTHOR

A Man Raised From the Bed of Death

One morning I received a phone call from my good friend, Paul. He told me that he knew of a man who owned a logging company and lumber yard who was about to die. They were waiting for him to expire any moment because his body was filled with cancer. Most of it was concentrated in his chest and spread out through the rest of his body. He was located in the McConnellsburg hospital. Paul asked me if I would be willing to go pray for him. I asked him to give me one day to fast and pray for this particular situation. I spent the rest of that day in prayer, fasting, and in the Word.

The next morning Paul came to pick me up. We drove up to the hospital, praying as we went. We walked into the foyer and up to the information desk. The nurse gave us the necessary information we needed. Paul said he would wait for me and that he would continue in prayer in the hospital's chapel. I found the room where they had put this gentleman, knocked on the door, and entered. They had placed him in a very small room—just big enough to be a closet—that was off the beaten path, like they were just waiting for him to die. He was lying on a hospital bed and was nothing but skin and bones; he looked as if he had just come out of a concentration camp. His skin and the whites of his eyes were yellow. He was a rather tall man who looked to be in his late sixties. He was lying on his bed wide awake. I had no idea what his mental condition was. I began to speak to him and discovered he was totally aware of his surroundings. Actually, I was amazed at how clear and quick his mind was.

I began to speak to him by introducing myself. He seemed to take an antagonistic attitude towards me right away. I began to share Jesus with him. As I was speaking to him, a smirk appeared on his face. He began to tell me stories of the things he had seen in church— supernatural things. He said one time he was in a wild church service where everybody was jumping and shouting. It was quite a number of years ago, and they did not yet have electricity in this church. He said as he was watching people dance and shout, one of them jumped so high that he hit a lighted kerosene lantern, causing it to fall off of the hook. It came crashing down onto the floor and should have immediately broken into pieces and caught the building on fire. Instead, he said it almost acted like a ball. It never broke or went out but landed straight up. The people just kept on dancing and singing to the Lord.

After he told me this story he looked me right in the eyes and said to me, "If I did not get saved back then, what makes you think you are going to get me saved now?"

I did not answer him. My heart was filled with deep sorrow and compassion for him. I knew I could not help him. I simply stepped away from his deathbed. I bowed my head and cried out to God. "Lord, help me to reach this man. I cannot do it within myself. Lord, You're going to have to touch his heart or he will lose his soul and end up in hell." As I was praying under my breath

I sensed the awesome presence of God flooding into that little hospital room.

Then the Spirit of the Lord rose up within me. I began to speak to this man under the unction of the Holy Ghost. I know I did not say very much. All of a sudden while I was speaking, he began to weep with tears shooting from his tear ducts. In just a matter of seconds his heart was completely open to the gospel. He gave his heart to Jesus Christ right then and there. Then I laid my hands on him and commanded his body to be healed. I rebuked the spirit of death and cancer in the name of Jesus Christ of Nazareth.

When I was done praying, it seemed to me there was some improvement. I told him I would visit him again in the hospital. After I left something wonderful happened. I did not hear the story until later. Immediately he felt healed in his body. His appetite came back and the yellow jaundice disappeared completely from his skin and eyes. The hospital personnel were amazed at this transformation. They took some new x-rays and discovered that the cancer he had in his body was almost totally gone. The cancer that was in his lungs which had been the size of a baseball was now the size of a cashew nut. In three days they released him from the hospital and sent him home. He was working at his sawmill with his son and grandsons within a week! We went to his house to eat a wonderful meal with his wife, son, his wife and grandchildren.

CHAPTER SEVEN

From the sermon: The Discerning of Spirits

#115　　I arrived one night at Gottenberg in Sweden and was asked to hold a meeting there. In the midst of the meeting a man fell full length in the doorway. The evil spirit drew him down, manifesting itself and disturbing the whole meeting. I rushed to the door and laid hold of this man and cried out to the evil spirit within him, "Come out, you devil! In the name of Jesus we cast you out as an evil spirit." I lifted him up and said, "Stand on your feet and walk in the name of Jesus." I don't know whether anybody in the meeting understood me except the interpreter, but the devils knew what I said. I talked in English but these devils in Sweden cleared out. A similar thing happened in Christiania.

Smith - It is impossible to overestimate the importance of being filled with the Spirit

#116　　At one time there was brought to me a beautiful young woman who had been fascinated with some preacher, and just because he had not taken interest in her on the line of courtship and marriage, the devil took advantage and made her fanatical and mad. They brought her 250 miles in that condition. She had previously received the Baptism in the Spirit. You ask, "can a demon come in to a person that has been baptized in the Holy Ghost?" Our only place of safety is if we are going on with God and in constantly being filled with the Holy Ghost. You must not forget Demas. He must have been baptized with the Holy Ghost for he appears to have been a right-hand worker with Paul, but the enemy got him to the place where he loved this present world and he dropped off. When they brought this young woman to me the evil power was immediately discerned and immediately I cast this demonic thing out in the name of Jesus. It was a great joy to present her before all the people in her right mind again. The devil has no power against the name of Jesus.

Smith - The greatest weakness of a preacher is when he draws men to himself.

#117   In Australia I went to one place where there were disrupted and broken homes. The people were so deluded by the evil power of Satan that men had left their wives, and wives had left their husbands, and had gotten into relationships with one another. That is the devil ! May God deliver us from such evils in these days. There is no one better than the companion God has already given you. I have seen so many broken hearts and so many homes that have been wrecked. We need a real revelation of these evil seducing spirits which come in and fascinate by the eye and destroy the lives of believers, and bring the work of God into disrepute. But there is always flesh behind these relationships. It is never pure or holy; it is unholy, impure, Satanic, devilish, and hell is behind it.

#118   I was at a meeting in Paisley in Scotland and came in touch with two young women. One of them wore a white blouse but it was smeared with blood. They were in a great state of excitement. These two girls were telegraph operators and were precious young women, having received the Baptism in the Spirit. They were both longing to be missionaries. But whatever our spiritual state is we are subject to temptations. An evil power came to one of these young women and said, "If you will obey me, I will make you one of the most wonderful missionaries that ever went out." This was just the devil or one of his agents acting as an angel of light. One of these young women was taken over immediately and she became so fanatical that her sister saw there was something wrong and asked the overseer to allow them to have a little time off.

As she took her into a room, the power of Satan, endeavoring to imitate the Spirit of God, manifested itself in a voice, and led this young woman to believe that the missionary enterprise would be unfolded that night if she would obey. This evil spirit said, "Don't tell anybody but your sister." I reckon that everything of God can be told everybody. If you cannot preach what you live, your life is wrong. If you are afraid of telling what you do in secret, someday it will be told from the housetop. Don't think that it will be kept a secret. That which is pure cometh to the light. He that doeth truth cometh to the light that his deeds may be made manifest, that they are wrought in God.

The evil power went on to say to this girl, "You go to the railroad station tonight, and there will be a train coming in at 7 :32. Buy a ticket for yourself and your sister. Then you will have six pence left. You will find a woman in a carriage dressed as a nurse, and opposite her will be a gentleman who has all the money you need." She bought her ticket and had just six pence left. The first thing came right. Next, the train came in at exactly 7:32. But the next thing did not come. They ran from the top to the bottom of that railroad train before it moved out and nothing turned out as they had been told. As soon as the train left the same voice came and said, "Over on the other platform." All that night until 9:30 p.m. these two young women were rushed from platform to platform. As soon as it was 9:30 this same evil power said, "Now that I know you will obey me, I will make you the greatest missionaries that have ever lived." Always something big! They might have known it was all wrong. This evil power said, "This gentleman will take you to a certain bank at a certain corner in Glasgow where he will give all that money to you." Banks are not open at that time of night in Glasgow. If she had gone to the street this evil spirit mentioned, there probably would not have been a bank there. All they needed was a little common sense and they would have seen that it was not the Lord. If you have your heart open for these kind of voices you will soon get into a trap. We must ever remember that there are many evil spirits in the world.

Were these two people delivered? Yes, after terrible travail with God, they were perfectly delivered. Their eyes were opened to see that this thing was not of God but of the devil. These two sisters are now laboring for the Lord in China and doing a blessed work for Him. If you do get into error on these lines, praise God there is a way out. I praise God that He will break us down till all pride leaves us. The worst pride we can have is the pride of exaltation of self.

Smith - As we think about that which is Holy, we become Holy. The more we think about Jesus, the more we become like Him.

#119   I knew some people who had a wonderful farm, very productive, in a very good neighborhood. They listened to voices telling them to sell everything and go to Africa. These voices so rushed them that they barely had time to sell out. They sold their property at a ridiculous low price. The same voices told them of a certain ship they were to sail on. When they got to the port they found there wasn't a ship of that name. The difficulty was this trying to get them not to believe these false voices were not of God. They said perhaps it was the mind of the Lord to give them another ship, and the voice soon gave them the name of another ship. When they reached Africa they knew no language that was spoken there. But the voice drove them almost to total self-destruction. They had to come back, brokenhearted, shaken down to nothing, and having lost all confidence in everything. If only these people would have had enough sense to go to some men of God who were filled with the Spirit and seek their counsel, they would soon have been persuaded that these voices were not of God. But listening to these voices always brings about a spiritual pride that makes a man or woman think that they are superior to their brethren, and that they are above taking counsel of men who they think are not so filled with the Spirit as they are. If you hear any voices that make you think that you are spiritually superior to those whom God has put in the church to rule the church, watch out, that is surely the devil.

Smith - Move in the realm of faith. Live in the realm of faith. Let God have His way!

Sermon: The Gift of Tongues

#120   Minister raised from the bed of death because a women spoke in tongues!

On this line I want to tell you about Willie Burton, who is laboring for God in the Belgium Congo. Brother Burton is a mighty man of God and is giving his life for the lost souls of Africa. He took fever and went down to death. They said; "He has preached his last; what shall we do?" All their hopes seemed to be destroyed, and there they stood, with broken hearts, wondering what was going to take place. They left him for dead; but, in a moment, without any signal, he stood right up in the midst of them completely healed; and they could not understand how it happened.

The explanation he gave was this, that, when he came to himself, he realized a warmth going right through his body; the next thing he knew there wasn't one thing wrong with him. How did it come about? It was a mystery until he went to London and was telling the people how he was left for dead, and then was raised up. A lady came up and asked for a private. conversation with him, and arranged a time. She asked, "Do you keep a diary?" He answered, "Yes." She told him,

"It happened on a certain day that I went to pray; and as soon as I knelt, I had you on my mind. -The Spirit of the Lord took hold of me and prayed through me in an unknown tongue. A vision came before me in which I saw you laid out helpless; and I cried out in the unknown tongue till I saw you rise up and go out of that room." She had kept a note of the time and when he turned to his diary he found that it was exactly the time when he was raised up. There are great possibilities as we yield to the Spirit and speak unto God in quiet hours in our bedrooms. God wants you to be filled with the Holy Ghost so that everything about you shall be charged with the dynamic of heaven.

Smith - None of you can be strong in God unless you are diligently & constantly listening to what He has to say through His Word.

#121   After receiving the Baptism in the Holy Ghost and speaking in tongues as the Spirit gave utterance, I did not speak with tongues again for nine months. I was troubled about it because I went up and down laying hands upon people that they might receive the Holy Ghost, and they were speaking in tongues, but I did not have the joy of speaking in tongues myself. God wanted to show me that the speaking in tongues as the Spirit gave utterance, which I received when I received the Baptism, was distinct from the gift of tongues which I received at a later date. When I laid hands on other people and they received the Holy Ghost, I used to think, "Oh, Lord Jesus, it would be nice if You would let me speak." He withheld the gift from me, for He knew that I would meet many who would say that the Baptism of the Holy Ghost can be received without the speaking in tongues, and that people simply received the gift of tongues when they received the Baptism.

I did not receive the gift of tongues at that time, but nine months later I was going out of the door one morning, speaking to the Lord in my own heart, when there came out of my mouth a new tongue. When the tongues stopped I said to the Lord, "Now, Lord, I did not do it, and I wasn't seeking it; so You have done it, and I am not going to move from this place until you give me the interpretation." And then came an interpretation which has been fulfilled all the world over. Is it the Holy Ghost who speaks? Then the Holy Ghost can interpret. Let him that speaks in a unknown tongue pray that he may interpret, and God will give the interpretation. We must not rush through without getting a clear understanding of what God has to say to us by his supernatural gifts, which are given by the Holy Ghost.

Smith - "God has ordained this speaking in an unknown tongue unto Himself as a wonderful, supernatural means of communication in the Spirit."

#122 There are many who call themselves believers who are extremely unbelieving. One of the unbelieving "believers" was a Methodist minister who lived in Sheffield, England. A man gave him a some money and told him to go and take a rest. This man also gave him my name and address; so, when he got to Bradford, he began to inquire about me. He was warned against me as one of the "tongues people," and was told to be very careful and not to be taken in by these false teachings, for the whole thing was of the devil. He said, "They will not deceive ME in; I know too much for them to deceive me."

He was quite worn out and needed rest; and when he came he said, "A friend of yours sent me to see you, is it all right?" I replied, "Yes, you are welcome." But we could do nothing with that man. It was impossible. Talk? You never heard anyone talk like him. It was talk, talk, talk, talk. He would never shut up. I said, "Let him alone, he will surely finish talking someday." We had dinner, and he talked through dinner time; we had the next meal and he talked through that.

It was our Friday night meeting for those seeking the Baptism of the Holy Ghost and the room began to be fill with people and still he talked. No one could get an edge in. He lodged himself in a place where he could not be disturbed by those coming in. I said, "Brother, you will have to stop now, we are going to pray." As a general thing we had some singing before going to prayer; but this time it was different. It was God's order. We got straight to prayer and as soon as we began to pray two young women, one on this side and the other on the other side began speaking in tongues. And this minister-it was all so strange to him-moved from one to the other to hear what they were saying. In a little while he said, "May I go to my room?" I said, "Yes, brother, if you wish." So he went to his room and we had a wonderful time.

We went to bed about eleven o'clock or so and at half-past three in the morning this man came to my bedroom door. Knock, knock, "May I come in?" "Yes, come in." He opened the door and said, "He is come, He is come"-holding his mouth, for he could hardly speak in English. I said, "Go back to bed, tell us tomorrow." Tongues are for the unbeliever, and this man was an unbeliever, an unbelieving "believer." Again and again I have seen conviction come upon people through the speaking in tongues.

The next morning he came down to breakfast and said, "Oh, was not that a wonderful night?" He said, "I know Greek and Hebrew, and those two young women were speaking these languages, one was saying in Greek, `Get right with God,' and the other was saying the same thing in Hebrew. I knew it was God speaking, and I knew it was not them speaking it. I first had to repent. I came in an unbeliever, but I found that God was here. - In the night God laid me on the floor for about two hours. I was helpless. Then God broke through." Here he began again to speak in tongues, right over the breakfast table.

Smith - God wants your life to manifest His glory!

Sermon: The God Who is Over All

The Devil is against the living Christ and wants to destroy Him; if you are filled with the living Christ, the Devil is eager to get you out of the way in order to destroy Christ's power. Say this to the Lord: "Now, Lord, look after this property of yours." Then the Devil cannot get near you. When does he get near? When you dethrone Christ, ignoring His rightful position over you, in you, and through you.

Sermon: The place of power

God is looking, God is wanting men and women who are willing to submit, and SUBMIT, and SUBMIT, and yield, and YIELD, and YIELD to the Holy Spirit until their bodies are saturated and soaked through and through with God, until you realize that God your Father has you in such condition that at any moment He can reveal His will to you and communicate whatever He wants to say to you.

God wants us to be in a place where the least breath of heaven makes us all on fire, ready for everything. You say, "How can I have that?" Oh, you can have that as easy as anything. "Can I?" Yes, it is as simple as possible. "How?" Let heaven come in; let the Holy Ghost take possession of you, and when He comes into your body you will find out that that is the keynote of the spirit of joy and the spirit of rapture, and if you will allow the Holy Ghost to have full control you will find you are living in the Spirit, and you will find out that the opportunities will be God's opportunities, and there is a difference between God's opportunities and ours. You will find you have come to the right place at the right time, and you will speak the right word at the right time and in the right place, and you will not go a warfare at your own charge.

Sermon: The Power of Christ's Resurrection.

#123   One morning about eleven o'clock I saw a woman who was suffering with a tumor. She would be dead before the end of the day. A little blind girl led me to her bedside. Compassion overwhelmed me and I wanted that woman to live for the child's sake. I said to the woman, "Do you want to live?" She could not speak. She just moved her finger. I anointed her with oil and said, "In the name of Jesus." There was a stillness of death that followed; and the pastor, looking at the woman, said to me, "She is gone."

When God pours in His compassion it has resurrection power in it. I carried that woman across the room, put her against a wardrobe, and held her there. I said, "In the name of Jesus, spirit of death, come out." And soon her body began to tremble like a leaf. "In Jesus' name, walk," I said. I stepped away from her body. She did walk and went back to bed.

I told this story in the assembly. There was a doctor there and he said, I am going to investigate this story." He went to the woman this happened to and she told him it was perfectly true. She said, "I was in heaven, and I saw countless numbers all like Jesus. Then I heard a voice saying, 'Walk, in the name of Jesus.'"

There is power in the name of Jesus. Let us apprehend it, the power of His resurrection, the power of His compassion, the power of His love. Love will overcome the most difficult situations - there is nothing it cannot conquer.

Smith - When you stay still, the devil will not disturb you. But when you press on, you are a target. But God will vindicate you.

Sermon: The Power of the Name

#124   One day I went up into the mountain to pray. I had a wonderful day. It was one of the high mountains of Wales. I heard of one man going up this mountain to pray, and the Spirit of the Lord met him so wonderfully that his face shone like that of an angel when he came back. Everyone in the village was talking about it. As I went up to this mountain and spent the day in the presence of the Lord, His wonderful power seemed to envelop, saturate, overwhelm and fill me.

Two years before this time there had come to our house two lads from Wales. They were just ordinary lads, but they became very zealous for God. They came to our mission and saw some of the works of God. They said to me, "We would not be surprised if the Lord brings you down to Wales to raise up our Lazarus." They explained that the leader of their assembly was a man who had spent his days working in a tin mine and his nights preaching, and the result was that he had collapsed, gone into consumption, and for four years he had been a helpless invalid, having to be fed with a spoon.

While I was up on that mountain top I was reminded of the transfiguration scene, and I felt that the Lord's only purpose in taking us into the glory was to fit us for greater usefulness in the valley. Now as I was on this mountain top that day, the Lord said to me, "I want you to go and raise Lazarus." I told the brother who accompanied me what the Lord told me, and when we got down to the valley, I wrote a postcard: "When I was up on the mountain praying today, God told me that I was to go and raise Lazarus." I addressed the postcard to the man in the place whose name had been given to me by the two lads.

When we arrived at the place we went to the man to whom I had addressed the card to. He looked at me and said, "Did you send this?" I said, "Yes." He said, "Do you think we believe in this? Here, take it." And he threw it at me.

The man called a servant and said, "Take this man and show him Lazarus." Then he said to me, "The moment you see him you will be ready to go home. Nothing will keep you here then." Everything he said was true from the natural viewpoint. The man was completely helpless. He was nothing but a mass of bones with skin stretched over them. There was no life to be seen at all. Everything in him spoke of decay and death.

I said to him, "Will you shout? You remember that at Jericho the people shouted while the walls were still up. God has the same type of victory for you if you will only believe." But I could not get him to believe not even an ounce. There was not an atom of faith in his heart. He had decided in his mind that there was no hope.

It is a blessed thing to learn that God's word can never fail. Never hearken to human plans or ideals. God can work mightily when you persist in believing Him in spite of discouragements from the human standpoint. When I got back to the man to whom I had sent the post-card, he asked, "Are you ready to go now?"

I told him I am not moved by what I see. I am moved only by what I believe. I know this for a fact that no man who was walking by faith looks at the circumstances if he believes. No man considers how he feels if he believes. The man who believes God has victory in every situation. Every man who comes into the fullness of the spirit can laugh at all things and believe God. There is something in the full gospel work that is different from anything else in the world. Somehow, in Pentecost, you know that God is a reality. Wherever the Holy Ghost has His way, the gifts of the Spirit will be in manifestation; and where these gifts are never in manifestation, I question whether He is present. Holy Ghost people are spoiled for anything else than Holy Ghost meetings. We want none of the entertainments that the churches are offering. When God comes in He entertains us Himself. Entertained by the King of kings and Lord of lords! O, it is wonderful.

There were spiritually difficult conditions in that Welsh village, and it seemed impossible to get the people to believe. "Ready to go home?" I was asked. But a man and a woman there asked us to come and stay with them. I said, "I want to know how many of you people can pray." No one wanted to pray. I asked if I could get seven people to pray with me for the poor man's deliverance. I said to the two people who were going to entertain us, "I will count on you two, and there is my friend and myself, and we need three others." I told the people that I trusted that some of them would awaken to their responsibility and come in the morning and join us in prayer for the raising of Lazarus. It will never do to give way to human opinions. If God says a thing, you are to believe it. Never even asked people what they think, because all the abundance of their heart they will utter their unbelief.

I told the people that I would not eat anything that night. When I went to bed it seemed as if the devil tried to place on me everything that he had placed on that poor man in the bed. When I awoke I had a cough and all the weakness of a tubercular patient. I rolled out of bed on to the floor and cried out to God to deliver me from the power of the devil. I shouted loud enough to wake everybody in the house, but nobody was disturbed. God gave me wonderful victory, and I got back into bed again as free as ever I was in my life. At 5 o'clock the Lord awakened me and said to me, "Don't break bread until you break it round my table." At 6 o'clock He gave me these words, "And I will raise him up." I put my elbow into the fellow who was sleeping with me. He said, "Ugh!" I put my elbow into him again and said, "Do you hear? The Lord says that He will raise Lazarus up."

At 8 o'clock they said to me, "Have a little refreshment." But I have found prayer and fasting the greatest joy, and you will always find it so when you are led by God. When we went to the house where Lazarus lived there were eight of us altogether. No one can prove to me that God does not always answer prayer. He always does more than we ask or think. He always gives exceedingly abundant above all we ask or think.

I shall never forget how the power of God fell on us as we went into that sick man's room. O, it was lovely! As we circled round the bed I got one brother to hold one of the sick man's hands and I held the other; and we each held the hand of the person next to us. I said, "We are not going to pray, we are just going to use the name of Jesus." We all knelt down and whispered that one word, "Jesus! Jesus! Jesus!" The power of God fell and then it lifted. Five times the power of God fell and then it remained. But the person who was in the bed was unmoved. Two years previous someone had come along and had tried to raise him up, and the devil had used his lack of success as a means of discouraging him. I said, "I don't care what the devil says; if God says he will raise you up it must be so. Forget everything else except what God says about Jesus."

The sixth time the power fell and the sick man's lips began moving and the tears began to fall. I said to him, "The power of God is here; it is yours to accept it." He said, "I have been bitter in my heart, and I know I have grieved the Spirit of God. Here I am helpless. I cannot lift my hands, nor even lift a spoon to my mouth." I said, "Repent, and God will hear you." He repented and cried out, "O God, let this be to Thy glory." As he said this the virtue of the Lord went right through him.

I have asked the Lord to never let me tell this story except as it was, for I realize that God cannot bless exaggerations. As we again said, "Jesus! Jesus! Jesus!" the bed shook, and the man shook. I said to the people that were with me, "You can all go down stairs right away. This is all God. I'm not going to assist him." I sat and watched that man get up and dress himself. We sang the doxology as he walked down the steps. I said to him, "Now tell what has happened."

It was soon noised abroad that Lazarus had been raised up from the bed of death and the people came from Llanelly and all the district around to see him and hear his testimony. God brought salvation to many. This man preached right out in the open air what God had done, and as a result many were convicted and converted. All this came through the name of Jesus, through faith in His name, yea, the faith that is by Him gave this sick man perfect soundness in the presence of them all.

Smith - Jesus bore my sins and sicknesses. If I dare believe, then I am justified. If I dare believe, then I am healed.

#125   I was one day preaching about the name of Jesus and there was a man leaning against a lamp-post, listening. It took a lamp-post to enable him to keep on his feet because he was so drunk. We had finished our open-air meeting, and the man was still leaning against the post. I asked him, "Are you sick?" He showed me his hand and I saw beneath his coat, he had a silver handled dagger. He told me that he was on his way to kill his unfaithful wife, but that he had heard me speaking about the power of the name of Jesus and could not get away. He said that he felt just helpless. I said, "Get you down." And there on the square, with people passing up and down, he got saved.

I took him to my home and put on him a new suit. I saw that there was something in that man that God could use. He said to me the next morning, "God has revealed Jesus to me; I see that all has been laid upon Jesus." I lent him some money, and he soon got together a wonderful little home. His faithless wife was living with another man, but he invited her back to the home that he had prepared for her. She came: and, where enmity and hatred had been before, the whole situation was transformed by love the love of God. God made that man a minister wherever he went. There is power in the name of Jesus everywhere. God can save to the uttermost.

Smith - Right now, the precious blood of Jesus Christ is efficacious to cleanse your heart & bring this wonderful life of God in you.

#126   We had a meeting in Stockholm that I shall ever bear in mind. There was a home for incurables there and one of the inmates was brought to the meeting. He had palsy and was shaking all over. He stood up before 3,000 people and came to the platform, supported by two others. The power of God fell on him as I anointed him in the name of Jesus. The moment I touched him he dropped his crutch and began to walk in the name of Jesus. He walked down the steps and round that great building in view of all the people. There is nothing that our God cannot do. He will do everything if you will dare to believe. Someone said to me, "Will you go to this Home for Incurables?" They took me there on my rest day. They brought out the sick people into a great corridor and in one hour the Lord set about twenty of them free. The name of Jesus is so marvelous.

Smith - All things are possible through the name of Jesus. There is power to overcome everything in the world through His name.

TEACHING FROM SMITH WIGGLESWORTH

ALL FALSE RELIGIONS WILL EMBRACE THE MAN OF SIN!

The "Man of Sin" as 'he comes forth will do many things. There will be many false Christ's and they will be manifestations of the forthcoming of the Man of Sin, but they will all come to an end. There will be the Man of Sin made, manifest.

These people are determined to have a man. They know someone has to come. They will polish him up as much as they can, and they will make him appealing in appearance, for we know that we are told by the Lord that those that go in soft clothing are simply wolves disguised like sheep.

What will make you to know it is the Man of Sin?

This: Every religious sect and creed there is in the world all joins to it. Romanism you see joined up with it. Buddhism joined with it. There is not a religion known but what is joined up to it.

That is exactly what the devil will do to convince the masses. He will have all the false religions joining right up and the Man of Sin, when he comes, will be received with great applause even by the deceived church.

Who will be saved? Who will know the day? Who knows now the Man of Sin? Why, we that love Christ will know him, when he opens his mouth, when he writes through the paper, when we see his actions — we will know who he is.

What has the Man of Sin always said? Why, THERE IS No hell. The devil has always said that What does Christian Science and False religions say? No hell, no devil They are ready for him. The devil has always said no hell, no evil (that Jesus was not God come in the flesh). And these people are preparing, and they do not know it, for the Man of Sin.

We have to see that these days have to come before the Lord can come. There has to be ,a falling away. There has to be a manifestation in this day so clear, of such undeniable fact. I tell you, when they begin to build temples for the Man of Sin to come (but they don't know it), you know the day is at hand.

A person said to me, "You see, all these ministers must be right — look at the beautiful buildings. Look at all the people following them."

Yes, everybody can belong to it. You can go to any place of sin you like, you can go to any theater you like, you can go to any race course you like, you can be mixed up with the rest of the people in your life and still be a Christian. You can have the devil right and left and anywhere, and still belong be a Christian.

EXPERIENCES FROM THE AUTHOR

God Raised my son from the bed of Death as he was dying from rabies!

When my son Daniel was 16 years old in 2000, he brought home a baby raccoon. He wanted to keep this raccoon as a pet. Immediately, people began to inform me that this was illegal. I further learned that in order to have a raccoon in Pennsylvania, one had to purchase one from someone who was licensed by the state to sell them. The reason for this was because of the high rate of rabies carried among them. But stubbornness rose up in my heart against what they were telling me, and I ignored sound logic.

You see, I had a raccoon when I was a child. Her mother had been killed on the highway and left behind a litter of her little ones. I had taken one of the little ones and bottle-fed it, naming her Candy. I have a lot of fond memories of this raccoon, so when my son wanted this raccoon, against better judgment and against the law of the land, I said okay. I did not realize that baby raccoons could have the rabies virus lying dormant in them for months before it would manifest. I knew in my heart that I was wrong to give him permission to keep this raccoon. But, like so many when we are out of the will of God, we justify ourselves. We stubbornly ignore the price that we will have to pay because of our rebellion and disobedience.

Daniel named his little raccoon Rascal. And he was a rascal because he was constantly getting into everything. A number of months went by and one night my son Daniel told me that he had a frightening dream. I should've known right then and there that we needed to get rid of this raccoon. He said in his dream, Rascal grew up and became big like a bear and then attacked and devoured him.

Some time went by and my son Daniel began to get sick, running a high fever. One morning, he came down telling me that something was majorly wrong with Rascal. He said that he was wobbling all over the place and was bumping into stuff. Immediately, the alarm bells went off. I asked him where his raccoon was. He informed me that Rascal was in his bedroom. Immediately I went upstairs to his room, opening his bedroom door. And their Rascal was acting extremely strange. He was bumping into everything and had spittle coming from his mouth.

Immediately, my heart was filled with great dread. I had grown up around wildlife and farm animals. I had run into animals with rabies before. No ifs, ands or buts, this raccoon had rabies. I immediately went to Danny asking him if the raccoon had bitten him or if he had gotten any of Rascal's saliva in his wounds? He showed me his hands where he had cuts on them, informing me that he had been letting rascal lick these wounds. He had even allowed rascal to lick his mouth.

Daniel did not look well and was running a high grade fever. He also informed me that he felt dizzy. I knew in my heart that we were in terrible trouble. I immediately called up the local forest ranger. They put me on the line with one of their personnel that had a lot of expertise in this area. When I informed him of what was going on, he asked me if I was aware of the fact that it was illegal to take in a wild raccoon. I told him I did know but that I had chosen to ignore the law.

He said that he would come immediately over to our house to examine this raccoon and if necessary to take it with him. I had placed Rascal in a cage making sure that I did not touch him. When the forest ranger arrived, I had the cage sitting in the driveway. He examined the raccoon without touching it. You could tell that he was quite concerned about the condition of this raccoon. He looked at me with deep regret informing me that in his opinion with 30 years wildlife service experience, this raccoon definitely had rabies. He asked me if there was anyone who had been in contact with this raccoon with any symptoms of sickness. I informed him that for the last couple days my son Daniel had not feeling well. As a matter of fact, he was quite sick. When I told him the symptoms that Daniel was experiencing, it was quite obvious the ranger was shaken and quite upset. He told me that anybody who had been in contact with this raccoon would have to receive shots. He went on to explain that from the description of what my son Daniel was going through and considering the length of his illness, it was too late for him! He literally told me that he felt from his experience that there was no hope for my son. He fully believed that my son would die from rabies. He loaded the raccoon up in the back of his truck, leaving me standing in my driveway weeping. He said that he would get back to me as soon as they had the test results and that I should get ready for state officials to descend upon myself, my family and our church.

I cannot express to you the hopelessness and despair that had struck my heart at that moment. Just earlier in the spring, our little girl Naomi had passed on to be with the Lord at 4 ½ years old. And now my second son Daniel was dying from rabies. Both of these situations could've been prevented.

Immediately, I gathered together my wife, my first son Michael, my third son Steven, and my daughter Stephanie. We all gathered around Daniel's bed and began to cry out to God. We wept, cried, and prayed crying out to God. I was repenting and asking God for mercy. Daniel, as he was lying on the bed running a high fever and almost delirious, informed me that he was barely able to hang on to consciousness. He knew in his heart, he said, that he was dying!

After everyone disbursed from his bed with great overwhelming sorrow, I went into our family room where we had a wood stove. I opened up the wood stove which still had a lot of cold ashes from the winter. Handful after handful of ashes I scooped out of the stove, pouring it over my head and saturating my body, with tears of repentance and sorrow running down my face. And then I lay in the ashes. The ashes got into my eyes, mouth and nose and into my lungs, making me quite sick. But I did not care, all that mattered was that God would have mercy on us and spare my son and all our loved ones from the rabies virus. As I lay on the floor in the ashes, crying out to God with all I had within

me, one could hear the house was filled with weeping, c.
praying family members.

All night long I wept and prayed,(about 16 hours) ask.
God to please have mercy on my stupidity. To remove the rat
virus not only from my son but from everyone else that had bec
contact with this raccoon. I also asked God to remove the virus
from Rascal as a sign that he had heard my prayers. I continued in
this state of great agony and prayer until early in the morning when
suddenly, the light of heaven shined upon my soul. Great peace
that passes understanding overwhelmed me. I got up with victory
in my heart and soul.

I went upstairs to check on my son Daniel. When I walked
into his bedroom, the presence of God was tangible. The fever had
broken and he was resting peacefully. Our whole house was filled
with the tangible presence of God. From that minute forward, he
was completely healed. A couple of days later, I was contacted by
the state informing me that, to their amazement, they could find
nothing wrong with the raccoon.

God had supernaturally removed the rabies virus not only
from my son and those in contact with Rascal, but from the
raccoon itself. Thank God that the Lord's mercy endures forever!

Dr Michael H Yeager

CHAPTER EIGHT

Sermon: The Word of Knowledge, and Faith

#127 I was in Ireland at one time and went to a house and said to the lady who came to the door, "Is Brother Wallace here?" She replied, "Oh, he has gone to Bangor, but God has sent you here for me. I need you. Come in." She told me her husband was a deacon of the Presbyterian Church. She had herself received the Baptism of the Holy Ghost while she was a member of the Presbyterian Church, but they did not accept it as from God. The people of the church said to her husband, "This thing cannot go on. We don't want you to be deacon any longer, and your wife is not wanted in the church." The man was very enraged and he became incensed against his wife. It seemed as though an evil spirit possessed him, and the home that had once been peaceful became very terrible: At last he left home and left no money behind him, and the woman asked me what should she do.

We went to prayer and before we had prayed five minutes the woman was mightily filled with the Holy Ghost. I said to her, "Sit down and let me talk to you. Are you often in the Spirit like this?" She said. "Yes, and what could I do without the Holy Ghost now?" I said to her, "The victory is yours. The Word of God says that you have power to sanctify your husband. Dare to believe the Word of God. Now the first thing we must do is to pray that your husband comes back tonight." She said, "I know he won't." I said, "If we agree together, it is done." She said, "I will agree." I said to her, "When he comes home show him all possible love, lavish everything upon him. If he will not listen what you have to say, let

163

him go to bed. The victory is yours. Get down before God and claim him for the Lord. Get into the glory just as you have got in today, and as the Spirit of God prays through you, you will find that God will grant all the desires of your heart."

A month later I saw this sister at a convention. She told how her husband came home that night and that he went to bed, but she prayed right through to victory and then laid her hands upon him. The moment she laid hands upon him he cried out for mercy. The Lord saved him and baptized him in the Holy Spirit. The power of God is beyond all our natural understanding or comprehension. The trouble is that we do not have the power of God in a full manifestation because of our limited minds, but as we go deeper and let God have His way, there is no limit to what our limitless God will do in response to a limitless faith. But you will never get anywhere except you are in constant pursuit of all the reality of God.

Smith - Voice your position in God and you will be surrounded by all the resources of God in the time of trial.

#128　　There are many that say they are believers but they are full of sickness and do not take a hold of the life of the Lord Jesus Christ that is provided for them. I was taken to see a woman who was dying and said to her, "How are you doing spiritually?" She answered, "I have faith, I believe." I said, "You know that you do not have faith, you know that you are dying. It is not faith that you have, it is mere mental acknowledgment." There is a difference between knowing something in your head and having faith. I saw that she was in the influence of the devil. There was no possibility of divine life until the enemy was removed from the premises. I hate the devil, and I laid hold of the woman and shouted, "Come out, you devil of death. I command you to come out in the name of Jesus." In one minute she stood on her feet in completely healed and in victory.

Smith - If you are not making people mad or glad, then there is something wrong with your ministry.

#129   I was at a camp meeting in Cazadero, California, several years ago, and a remarkable thing happened. A man came to the meeting who was stone deaf. I prayed for him and I knew that God had healed him. Then came the test. He would always move his chair up to the platform, and every time I got up to speak he would get up as close as he could and strain his ears to catch what I had to say. The devil said, "It isn't done." I declared, "It is done." This went on for three weeks and then the manifestation came and he could hear distinctly up to sixty yards away. When his ears were opened he thought it was so great that he had to stop the meeting and tell everybody about it. I met him in Oakland recently and he was hearing perfectly. As we remain steadfast and unmovable on the ground of faith, we shall see what we believe for in perfect manifestation.

Smith - See to it that nothing comes out of your lips that will interfere with the work of the Lord.

#130   The other day I was in San Francisco. I sat on a car and saw a boy in great agony on the street. I said, "Let me get out." I rushed to where the boy was. He was in agony through agonizing cramps of the stomach. I put my hands on his stomach in the name of Jesus. The boy jumped, and stared at me with astonishment. He found himself instantly free. The gift of faith dared in the face of everything. It is as we are in the Spirit that the Spirit of God will operate this gift anywhere and at any time.

#131   God cannot trust some with the gift, but only those who have a lowly, broken, contrite heart He can trust. One day I was in a meeting where there were a lot of doctors and eminent men, and many ministers. It was at a convention, and the power of God fell on the meeting. One humble little girl that waited at table opened her whole heart and being to the Lord and was immediately filled with the Holy Ghost and began to speak in tongues. All these 'big men stretched their necks and looked up to see what was happening and were saying, "Who is it?" Then they learned it was "the servant!" Nobody received but "the servant!" These things are hidden and kept back from the wise and prudent, but the little children, the lowly ones, are the ones that receive. We cannot have faith if we have honor one of another. A man who is going on with God won't accept honor from his fellow beings. God honors the man of a broken, contrite spirit. How shall I get there? So many people want to do great things, and to be seen doing them, but the one that God will use is the one that is willing to be hidden.

Smith - God wants you to be filled with all fulness, increasing with all increasings with measureless measures of the might of the Spirit!

#132   At one time I was in Lincolnshire in England and came in touch with the old pastor of an Episcopalian Church. He became much interested and asked me into his library. I never heard anything sweeter than the prayer the old man uttered as he got down to pray. He began to pray, "Lord, make me holy. Lord, sanctify me." I called out, "Wake up! Wake up now! Get up and sit in your chair." He sat up and looked at me. I said to him, "I thought you were holy." He answered, "Yes." "Then what makes you ask God to do what He has done for you?" He began to laugh and then to speak in tongues. Let us move into the realm of faith, and live in the realm of faith, and let God have His way.

Smith – If you preach faith, then you must live it!

Sermon: The Words of This Life

#133   I had been preaching at Stavanger in Norway, and was very tired and wanted a few hours rest. I went to my next appointment, arriving at about 9:30 in the morning. My first meeting was to be at night. I said to my interpreter, "After we have had something to eat, let us go down to the fjords." We spent three or four hours down by the sea and at about 4:30 returned. We found the end of the street, which has a narrow entrance, just filled with autos, wagons, etc., containing invalids and sick people of every kind. I went up to the house and was told that the house was full of sick people. It reminded me of the scene described in the fifth chapter of Acts. I began praying for the people in the street and God began to heal the people. How wonderfully He healed those people who were in the house. We sat down for a lunch and the telephone bell rang and someone at the other end was saying, "What shall we do? The town hall is already full; the police cannot control things."

In that little Norwegian town the people were jammed together, and oh, how the power of God fell upon us. A cry went up from every one, "Is this the revival?"

Revival is coming. The breath of the Almighty is coming. The breath of God shows up every defect, and as it comes flowing in like a river, everybody will need a fresh anointing, a fresh cleansing of the blood. You can depend upon it that that breath is upon us.

Smith - There are boundless possibilities for you if you dare to believe.

#134   At one time I was at a meeting in Ireland. There were many sick carried to that meeting and helpless ones were helped there. There were many people in that place who were seeking for the Baptism of the Holy Ghost. Some of them had been seeking for years. There were sinners there who were under mighty conviction. There came a moment when the breath of God swept through the meeting. In about ten minutes every sinner in the place was saved. Everyone who had been seeking the Holy Spirit was baptized, and every sick one was healed. God is a reality and His power can never fail. As our faith reaches out, God will meet us and the same rain will fall. It is the same blood that cleanses, the same power, the same Holy Ghost, and the same Jesus made real through the power of the Holy Ghost. What would happen if we should believe God?

Smith - Many want to be healed, but harbor things in their hearts. Let these things go. Forgive, and the Lord will forgive you.

#135   I was passing through the city of London one time, and Mr. Mundell, the secretary of the Pentecostal Missionary Union, learned that I was there. He arranged for me to meet him at a certain place at 3:30 p. m. I was to meet a certain boy whose father and mother lived in the city of Salisbury. They had sent this young man to London to take care of their business. He had been a leader in Sunday school work but he had been betrayed and had fallen. Sin is awful and the wages of sin is death. But there is another side-the gift of God is eternal life.

This young man was in great distress; he had contracted a horrible disease and feared to tell anyone. There was nothing but death ahead for him. When the father and mother got to know of his condition they suffered inexpressible grief.

When we got to the house, Brother Mundell suggested, that we get down to prayer. I said, "God does not say so, we are not going to pray yet. I want to quote a scripture, *`Fools, because of their transgression, and because of their iniquities, are afflicted: their soul abhorreth all manner of meat; and they draw near unto the gates of death.'"* The young man cried out, "I am that fool." He broke down and told us the story of his fall. Oh, if men would only repent, and confess their sins, how God would stretch out His hand to heal and to save. The moment that young man repented, a great abscess burst, and God sent virtue into his life, giving him a mighty deliverance and he was completely healed of that terrible disease.

Smith - The devil knows that if he can capture your thought life, he has won a mighty victory over you.

Sermon: What It Means to Be Full of the Holy Ghost

#136   When you are filled with the Spirit you will know the voice of God. I want to give you one illustration of this. When I was going out to Australia recently, our boat stopped at Aden and at Bombay. In the first place the people came round the ship selling their wares, beautiful carpets and all sorts of oriental things. There was one man selling some ostrich feathers. As I was looking over the side of the ship watching the trading, a gentleman said to me, "Would you go shares with me in buying that bunch of feathers?" What did I want with feathers? I had no use for such things and no room for them either. But the gentleman put the question to me again, "Will you go shares with me in buying that bunch?" The Spirit of God said to me, "Do it."

The feathers were sold to us for three pounds, and the gentleman said, "I have no money on me, but if you will pay the man for them, I will send the cash down to you by the purser." I paid for the feathers and gave the gentleman his share. He was traveling first, and I was traveling second class. I said to him, "No, please don't give that money to the purser, I want you to bring it to me personally to my cabin." I said to the Lord, "What about these feathers?" He showed me that He had a purpose in my purchasing them.

At about 10 o'clock the gentleman came to my cabin and said, "I've brought the money." I said to him, "It is not your money that I want, it is your soul that I am seeking for God." Right there he opened up the whole plan of his life and began to seek God; and that morning he wept his way through to God's salvation.

Smith - Out of the emptiness, brokenness & yieldedness of our lives, God can bring forth all His glories through us to others.

#137   At a meeting I was holding, the Lord was working and many were being healed. A man saw what was taking place and remarked, "I'd like to try this thing." He came up for prayer and told me that his body was broken in two places. I laid my hands on him in the name of the Lord, and said to him, "Now, you believe God." The next night he was at meeting and he got up like a lion. He said, "I want to tell you people that this man here is deceiving you. He laid his hands on me last night for a rupture in two places, but I'm not a bit better." I stopped him and said, "You are healed, your trouble is that you won't believe it."

He was at meeting the next night and when there was opportunity for testimony this man arose. He said, "I'm a mason by trade. Today I was working with a laborer and he had to put a big stone in place. I helped him and did not feel any pain. I said to myself, `How can this be possible?' I went away to a place where I could strip, and found that I was healed." I told the people, "Last night this man was not of God, but now I know I was completely wrong.

Smith - We never go wrong in exalting the Lord Jesus Christ, giving Him the preeminent place and magnifying Him as Lord and Christ.

Sermon: What wilt Thou have me to do?

#138   A woman came to me one day and said, "My husband is so difficult for me to live with; the minute he gets his paycheck he spends it on alcohol, and then he cannot do his work and comes home; I love him very much, what can be done?" I said, "If I were you I would take a handkerchief and would place it under his head when he went to sleep at night, and say nothing to him, but have a living faith." We anointed a handkerchief in the name of Jesus, and she put it under his head. Oh, beloved, there is a way to reach these wayward ones. The next morning on his way to work he called for a glass of beer; he lifted it to his lips, but he thought there was something wrong with it, and he put it down and went out. He went to another saloon, and another, and did the same thing. He came home sober. His wife was gladly surprised and he told her the story; how it had affected him. That was the turning point in his life; it meant not only giving up drink, but it meant his salvation.

Smith - A thankful heart is a receiving heart; God wants to keep you in the place of constant believing with thanksgiving so you will receive.

#139 A dear young Russian came to England. He did not know the language, but learned it quickly and was very much used and blessed of God; and as the wonderful manifestations of the power of God were seen, they pressed upon him to know the secret of his power, but he felt it was so sacred between him and God he should not tell it, but they pressed him so much he finally said to them: "First God called me, and His presence was so precious, that I said to God at every call I would obey Him, and I yielded, and yielded, and yielded, until I realized that I was simply clothed with another power altogether, and I realized that God took me, tongue, thoughts and everything, and I was not myself but it was Christ working through me." How many of you today have known that God has called you over and over, and has put His hand upon you, but you have not yielded in every area of your life? How many of you have had the breathing of His power within you, calling you to prayer, or the meditation of the word and you have to confess you have failed?

Smith - Faith is the audacity that rejoices in the fact that God cannot break His own Word!

#140 I went to a house one afternoon where I had been called, and met a man at the door. He said, "My wife has not been out of bed for eight months; she is completely paralyzed. She has been looking so much for you to come, she is hoping God will raise her up." I went in and rebuked the devil's power. She said, "I know I am healed; if you go out I will get up." I left the house, and went away not hearing anything more about her situation. I went to a meeting that night, and a man jumped up and said he had something he wanted to say; he had to go to catch a train but wanted to talk first. He said, "I come to this city once a week, and I visit the sick all over the city. There is a woman I have been visiting and I was very much in despair about her; she was completely paralyzed and has laid on that bed many months, and when I went there today she was up doing her work." I tell this story because I want you to see Jesus.

Smith - When we all (with one heart & one faith) believe the Word, then miracles will be manifested everywhere!

Sermon: Wilt Thou Be Made Whole?

#141 I visited a woman who had been suffering for many years. She was all twisted up with rheumatism and had been two years in this condition in bed. I said to her, "why are you laying here in this condition as a believer?" She said, "I've come to the conclusion that I have a thorn in the flesh." I said, "To what wonderful degree of righteousness or revelation have you attained that you have to have a thorn in the flesh? Have you had such an abundance of divine revelations that there is danger of your being exalted above measure ?" She said, "I believe it is the Lord who is causing me to suffer." I said, "You believe it is the Lord's will for you to suffer, and yet you are trying to get out God's will as quickly as you can. Look there are doctor's bottles all over the place.

It is time to get off your high and holy place and confess that you are a sinner. If you'll get rid of your self-righteousness, God will do something for you. Drop the idea that you are so holy that God has got to afflict you. Sin is the cause of your sickness and not righteousness. Disease is not caused by righteousness, but by sin."

There is healing through the blood of Christ and deliverance for every captive. God never intended His children to live in misery because of some affliction that comes directly from the devil. A perfect atonement was made at Calvary. I believe that Jesus bore my sins, and I am free from them all. I am justified from all things if I dare believe. He Himself took our infirmities and bare our sicknesses; and if I dare believe, I can be healed.

Smith - **If you will but believe, God will meet you and bring into your life the sunshine of His love.**

#142   I was in Long Beach, California, one day, with a friend, we were passing a hotel. He told me of a doctor there who had a diseased leg; that he had been suffering from it for six years, and could not get out. We went up to his room and found four doctors there. I said, "Well, doctor, I see you have plenty of help, I'll call again another day." I was passing that same hotel another time, and the Spirit said, "Go join thyself to him." Poor doctor! He surely was in a bad condition. He said, "I have been like this for six years, and nothing human can help me." I said, "You need God Almighty." People are trying to patch up their lives; but you cannot do anything without God. I talked to him for a while about the Lord, and then prayed for him. I cried, "Come out of him, in the name of Jesus." The doctor cried, "It's all gone!"

I was in Long Beach about six weeks later, and the sick were coming for prayer. Among those filling up the aisle was the doctor. I said, "What is the trouble now?" He said, "Diabetes, but it will be all right tonight. I know it will be all right.

At that meeting there was an old man helping his son to the altar. He said, "He has many seizures every day." Then there was a woman with a cancer. Oh, what sin has done! We read that, when God brought forth His people from Egypt, "there was not one feeble person among their tribes" (Ps. 105:37). No disease! All healed by the power of God! I believe that God wants a people like that today. All of these precious people including that Doctor was healed.

Smith - If you leave people as you found them, God has not spoken through you.

From the Pentecostal Evangel.

#143 A young woman declares: "I was brought to last Sunday's meeting a poor, dying woman, with a disease which was eating into every part of my being. I was full of corruption outside as well as in; but the Lord Jesus Christ came and loosed me and set me free. Since then I have slept better and have eaten more heartily than I have for eight years."

*The president of the Methodist Local Preachers' Association testified to having been delivered from nervous trouble.

Smith - Inactivity is a robber which steals blessings. Increase comes by action, by using what we have and know.

#144 Mr. Solglush, a prominent business man, testified to deliverance from an affliction in the feet since he was two years old; now he is fifty two. "Since I was prayed for in the name of Jesus all pain is gone. No one has ever seen me do this (stamping his feet). I have no use for my walking stick. Any longer."

Smith - You cannot bear with others until you know how God has borne with you.

#145   A lady said: "While sitting in in one of Mister Wigglesworth services, listening to the Word, God healed me of liver trouble, gall stones and sciatica. He has also touched my daughter who was suffering with her feet, having been operated on twice; she had little hope of being anything but an invalid the rest of her life; but the Lord operated. All pain has gone. She is no longer an invalid. Praise the Lord."

Smith - You open the way, by faith. Then God supplies your need, by grace.

#146   Mr. Lewellyn, a Church of England "Reader," testified to having been immediately healed of a stiff knee.

*Mr. Barrett testified that Miss Witt, of Box Hill, who has been 22 years in an invalid chair, rose and walked after Mr. Wigglesworth ministered to her in the name of Jesus.

*Another testified of having been healed the night before of rheumatoid arthritis of four years standing, discarding crutch and stick.

*Mr. Johnsone of Sperm Vale, who had been deaf twenty years, and his wife, who had sat in a wheelchair for six years, were immediately healed. The empty chair was wheeled to the railway station, the woman testifying to passersby of the great things God had done for her.

Smith - Voice your position in God and you will be surrounded by all the resources of God in the time of trial.

From the Pentecostal Evangel.

#147   I prayed for a sister who had cancer and she said, "I know I'm free and that God has delivered me." Then they brought the boy with the seizures, and I commanded the evil spirits to leave, in the name of Jesus. Then I prayed for the doctor. At the next night's meeting the house was full. I called out, "Now, doctor, what about the diabetes?" He said, "It has gone." Then I said to the old man, "What about your son?" He said, "He hasn't had any fits since." We have a God who answers prayer.

Smith - Discouraged one, cast your burden on the Lord. He will sustain you. Look unto Him and be lightened. Look unto Him now

TEACHING FROM SMITH WIGGLESWORTH

#Taught about the False Grace message that says you can live how you want as a believer and still be saved!

All the saints of God that get the real vision of this wonderful transformation are recognizing every day that the world is getting worse and worse and worse and ripening for judgment. And God is bringing us to a place where we which that are spiritual are having, a clear vision that we MUST at any cost PUT OFF the WORKS, of DARKNESSS. We must be getting ourselves ready for that glorious day when we see Christ.

These are the last days. What will be the strongest confirmation for me to bring to you the reality that we are living in the last days?

There are in the world **TWO CLASSES** of believers. There are believers which are disobedient, or I ought to say there are children which are saved by the power of God which are still choosing to live as DISOBEDIENT children. And then there are children which are just the same saved by the power of God but who all the time are longing to be MORE OBEDIENT.

In this fact Satan has a great part to play. It is on this factor in these last years that some of us have been brought to great grief at the first opening of the door with brazen fact to fleshly sinful forces. And we heard the word come rushing, like the wind to a, "new theology" that is damnable, devilish, evil power that teaches you can be disobedient children, and still be right with God.

As soon as this was noised abroad everywhere, this "new theology," everybody began to say, "What is this new theology?" It's an absolute live from the devil!

The spirit of this age is to get you to believe a lie. If you believe a lie, you cannot believe the truth When once you are seasoned with a lie against the Word of God, He sends you strong delusion that you shall believe a lie Who does? God is gracious over His Word His Word is from everlasting His Word is true.

When we see those things which are coming to pass, what do we know? We know the time is at hand. The fig tree is budding for these false prophets and these line spirits.

EXPERIENCES FROM THE AUTHOR

*My Family and I Was Saved from a Terrible Death At the Mississippi River!
(2007)

Many times in my life I have had vivid experiences, perceiving that God is about to do something or that something is about to take place right before it happens! Here is just one example.

On August 1, 2007 my wife, three sons, daughter and I were traveling on Highway I 35 West. We were in our Toyota crew cab pickup truck, pulling a 35 foot fifth wheel trailer. We were on vacation and headed for Yellowstone National Park. At the time, we were headed towards the downtown area of Minneapolis, Minnesota. As I was driving, I sensed in my heart that we needed to get off this highway even though our GPS was taking us the shortest route to where we were headed. I have discovered and personally experienced 20 major ways that God leads and guides. All 20 of these specific ways in which God leads and guides can be discovered in the Scriptures. What I felt is what I call a Divine unction of the Holy Ghost. It is more than a perception or a feeling. It is more like an overwhelming urgency that flows up out of your belly.

I informed my family that something definitely was wrong, that there was an urgency in my heart and we needed to get off this highway I 35 W. immediately. This is the only time that I have experienced the urgency to get off a road or highway like this. I took the nearest exit and went north towards Canada. After a while, we connected to another highway and headed west. Later in the day, we pulled into a store to take a break from driving. As we entered this facility, we noticed that there were people gathered around the TV.

We could see that some major disaster had taken place. The viewer's informed us that a bridge had collapsed over the Mississippi River earlier in the day with lots of traffic that was loaded on top of it. We could see cars, trucks, buses everywhere that had fallen into the Mississippi. Amazingly it was the highway the spirit of God Quicken my heart to get off of, it was I 35 W ! If I had not left the highway, we would have been on that bridge when it collapsed into the Mississippi River. Thirteen people died that day and (145) were seriously injured. Not including all of the terrible destruction, and horrible nightmare that took place with all of those who were a part of this tragedy. Only God knows if we would've died or not if I had not been obedient to that Holy Ghost unction.

*If I Had Not Heard from God, My Family and I Would've Been Swept Away When the Dam Broke at Dell Lake in Wisconsin! (2008)

On June 8, 2008 my family and I were in Wisconsin at Dell Lake ministering in special meetings for an Indian tribe called the Ho-Chunk Nation. We were there by their invitation. They had provided the facility, and all the advertisements. We had been having some wonderful services. It was the second night of these meetings. At the end of the service out of the blue I heard the voice of God say: pack up your camper and leave tonight! It had been a long day and my flesh sure did not want to leave, but I know the voice of God. I told the sponsors of the meetings that I was sorry but I would have to go back to Pennsylvania, tonight. I could tell they were extremely disappointed. They tried to convince me to stay because God was moving in such a wonderful way, but I know the voice of God.

My family members were also disappointed. They asked me why we were leaving? They reminded me that I have never canceled or shortened my commitments. I told them I understood this. But we had to leave tonight. I did not know why. I heard the Lord tell me we must leave tonight, so tonight we will leave. We arrived back at the Dell Lake camp grounds. It was beginning to rain extremely hard. My family asked if we could simply wait until the next morning because it was late, dark and raining heavily. I said no, we must go now! I backed my truck up to the fifth wheel trailer. I saw the spirit of God come upon my 2nd son Daniel, who does not like to get wet or even really work, begin to work frantically. I mean he really began to move like in the supernatural hurry. My boys and I connected up the 5th wheel camper, we picked up all of our equipment and drew in the extended sides of the trailer.

Everybody was wet and tired as we loaded into the crew cab Toyota truck. Then, we were on our way. I noticed as I drove past the Dell Lake dam that water was rushing by like a little river on both sides of the road. Some parts of the road were already flooded. We drove through the night. There were times we had to crawl because the rain was coming down so hard, fog and strong winds. All the way through Wisconsin, Illinois and Indiana, Ohio the rain came. The wind was extremely strong. We saw 18 wheelers turned over. Lots of car accidents. Trees and debris were blowing everywhere. And yet God was protecting us.

The next day when we had finally arrived back in Pennsylvania, we discovered some shocking news. There had been hundreds of twisters and tornadoes right behind us which caused a huge amount of devastation. But that wasn't the only news. The dam at Dell Lake, Wisconsin had completely and totally collapsed. Dell Lake is the largest man-made lake in Wisconsin, and this had never happened before in all of its history. The whole lake rushed out over the town. We would have been washed away in the storm. There is video footage of this disaster on the Internet.

CHAPTER NINE

A Report published in Confidence, p. 228-229 December 1914

#148   "I slipped and fell on Broadway, San Diego, in February, 1921 I discovered afterwards that I had fractured the base of my spine. I had so severely wrenched the hips and pelvic bones that I was filled with great pain from that moment forward. As the broken bone was not discovered and set until about two months after the accident, the constant pain and irritation caused a general inflammation of my nervous system, and the long delay in getting the bone set, made it impossible to heal, so that, my condition steadily grew worse, and I was taken to the hospital and the bone was removed about a month after it had been set. Though the wound healed rapidly, the nervous inflammation remained, and so for many months longer I was in constant pain and unable to get around without assistance. I was taken to the first service held by Mr. Wigglesworth on the 2nd of October, 1922. At the close of the service all those who were sick and in pain and had come for healing were requested to rise if possible. My husband assisted me to my feet, and as those were prayed for by Mister Wigglesworth in the name of Jesus Christ I was instantly healed. How I was healed I do not know. I only know the Great Physician touched my body and I was made whole, and freed from pain.

"After I got home I showed everyone how I could sit down and rise with my hands above my head; when before it had taken both hands to push up my feeble body, and I had to have straps on my bed to pull myself up by. No more use for them now! I lay down and turned over for the first time since the accident without pain. I shall never cease to praise God for the healing of my body through the precious blood of Jesus and in His name. I walked to the street car alone the next day and attended the next service and have been "on the go" ever since. To Jesus be all the, praise and glory." – Mrs. Sanders, 4051 Bay View Court, San Diego, Calif.

Smith - It is when we are at the end of our own resources that we can enter into the riches of God's resources.

#149   One day Smith and his wife received a letter from a young man asking for prayer. He had been healed about three years before of a bad foot, and they had lost all trace of him since, until this urgent cry came from a home where in the natural, death was soon to enter. When the letter came Mrs. Wigglesworth said to her husband, "If you go, God will give you this case." He telegraphed back that he would go. Wigglesworth got on his bicycle riding from Grantham, nine miles away to Willsford. When he reached the village he inquired where the young man, Matthew Snell, lived. This young man had heart failure and had to lie perfectly still in one place. The doctor said if he moved from that place he would surely die, and left him, never expecting to see him alive again. When Mr. Wigglesworth reached the house, the mother of the young man stood in the doorway and said, "Oh you have come too late." "Is he alive at all?" He asked the mother. "Yes, he is just barely alive."

Smith went into the parlor where he was lying. The young man, Matthew, said in a barely audible voice, "I cannot rise, I am too weak, and the doctor says if I turn around I shall die." Mr. Wigglesworth said this to him, "Matthew, the Lord is the strength of your heart and thy portion altogether. Will you believe that the Lord will raise you up for His glory?" The young man answered, "Lord, if You will raise me up for Your glory I will give You my life." Hands were laid on him in the name of the Lord Jesus Christ and instantly new life came into him. "Shall I arise?" he asked, but Wigglesworth felt in his heart that the young man should lie perfectly quiet and so advised. The night was spent in prayer and the next morning Brother Wigglesworth attended the ten o'clock meeting in the Primitive Methodist Chapel. He was asked to speak and talked of faith in God, and from that moment the unbelief seemed to clear away from the village people. They came to him at the close of the service and said, "We believe Matthew will be raised up." He had asked the family to air Matthew's clothing for him for that he could wear them, but they did not do it because they did not believe he would be healed. For six weeks he had been in a very serious condition, becoming weaker all the time. Mr. Wigglesworth strongly insisted on them preparing Matthew's clothes. They finally relented not because they believed for healing, but to satisfy him. About 2:30 he went into the room where the young man lay and said,

"Now I would like this to be for the glory of God. It shall never be said that Wigglesworth raised you up." The young man answered, "For Thy glory, Lord; my life shall be for Thee." Then the servant of the Lord said, "Matthew, I believe the moment I lay hands on you the glory of God will fill this place so I shall not be able to stand." As he did this the glory of the Lord fell upon them until he fell on his face to the floor; it increased until everything in the room shook, the bed and Matthew who was on the bed, and with a strong voice the young man cried out, "For Thy glory, Lord !" "For Thy glory!" This continued for at least fifteen minutes, when it was apparent to them God would give him strength not only to rise but to dress in the glorious power which seemed like the description given of the temple being filled with the glory of God, and the young man was walking up and down, shouting and praising God and clapping his hands.

He went to the door and called to his father that the Lord had raised him up. His father was a backslider and fell down before God and cried for mercy. His sister, who had been brought out of an asylum and was threatened with another attack of insanity, in the manifestation of that glory was delivered from that time. That weak body immediately became strong, eating regular food immediately. The doctor came and examined his heart and declared it was all right. Matthew declared it should be for the

Lord's glory and at once began preaching in the power of the Holy Ghost. His own statement is that when he gives the story of his healing many are saved.

Smith - When we get to the place where we take no thought of ourselves, then God takes thought for us.

#150 On Monday, after Matthew was healed, Mr. Wigglesworth started up the road with a brother, when the Lord said to him, "That woman with the apron on up the road is not saved." He mentioned to the brother the impression he had and when he neared the woman he said, "The Lord convinced me coming up the road that you do not know Him and that you want to be saved." Instantly she spoke out loudly that for three weeks she had been under conviction and wanted salvation. They went into the cottage across the way and God instantly saved her.

Going from there to Grantham to take the train he stopped to see the mother of a young woman who had been converted in their mission in Bradford. When he reached her house she said, "Don't stop here. Go with that man on his bicycle," pointing to a man some distance off. Before they reached the house they heard a voice crying out, "Oh, dear me!" "Oh, dear me!" When they got inside they found a man suffering terrible agony and distress. At first Brother Wigglesworth thought he was sent there that the man might be healed, but instead of that he asked, "Are you saved?" The sick man cried out, "I would give the world! I would die comfortable if I were." Brother Wigglesworth pointed him to the Way of salvation, rebuked the unbelief, and instantly the man realized that he had passed from death into life and the shout of joy took the place of the cry of distress. His wife, seeing the joy that came to her husband, fell down at his bedside and cried for salvation. He was not led to pray for the sick man's healing and in three hours he went sweeping through the gates of heaven.

Smith – I am not here to entertain you, but to get you to the place where you can laugh at the impossible!

#151 A friend of Smith's was dying. They had been kindred spirits from their boyhood days, perfect love existed between them. When Mr. Wigglesworth reached home one evening he found his wife had gone to see his friend who was sick and he immediately started down to see him also. As he neared the house he knew something serious had happened, and as he passed up the stairway he found the wife of the sick man lying on the stairs, broken-hearted. Death had already taken place. As he entered the room where the man lay, the deep love he had always cherished overcame him and he lost control of himself and began crying out to God. His wife who was present tried to constrain him, but as his heart went out to God he was lost to all around and felt he was being drawn up by the Spirit into the heavenlier. The deep cry of his heart was: "Father, Father, in Jesus' Name bring him back." He opened his eyes to find out there were no altered conditions, but with a living faith he cried out, "He lives! He lives! Look! Look!" The dead man opened his eyes and revived, and he is living still to the writing of this story.

Smith - See to it there is never anything comes out of your lips or by your acts that will interfere with the work of the Lord

#152   A young woman came into Smith's mission one night and was so impressed with what she heard that at the close she said to Mrs. Wigglesworth: "There is a young woman at Allerton who has been living there for six years and never been outside the door. Will you go up there?" Mrs. Wigglesworth referred her to her husband and he said he would go. As he started down the road, which was filled with people traveling to and fro, the Holy Ghost fell upon him so that he stood in the street and shouted for joy, and the tears rained down his face and saturated his waistcoat. To his astonishment, nobody in the street seemed to recognize his condition; it seemed as though the Lord covered him. He dared not speak to anybody lest the presence of the Lord should leave him. The young woman who went with him was full of talk, but he said nothing. As soon as he entered the house the glory of God came more fully upon him and as he lay hands on this poor afflicted woman the glory of God filled the house. He was so filled with God's glory he rushed out of the house and the young woman running after him exclaiming, "How did you get this glory? Tell me! Tell me!" He told her to go back into the house and seek the Lord.

A week after that he was in an office in Bradford and as soon as he entered the office a man said, "Wigglesworth, sit down. I want to tell you something." He sat down to listen, and the office-man said, "Last Sunday night at the chapel the preacher was in the midst of preaching when suddenly the door swung open, and in came a young woman who had been confined to her home for six years. She stood up and said that as she came out of the house the heavens were covered with the most glorious light and presence of God, and she read over the heavens. 'The Lord is coming soon.'" Mr. Wigglesworth wept and praised God, but said nothing. He realized that God wanted him to know the young lady had been healed but that he was not to talk about it.

Smith - Now hear this. Faith knows no defeat!

Report published in Confidence, p. 228-229 December 1914

#153   At Victoria Halt there came a woman pressed down with cancer of the breast. She was anointed with oil, according to God's Word. I laid hands on the cancer, cast out the demon, immediately the cancer which had up to then been bleeding, dried up. She received a deep impression through the Spirit that the work was done, and closely watched the healing process together with a lady friend. The cancer began to move from its seat, and in five days dropped out entirely into the protecting bandage. They were greatly blessed and full of joy, and when looking into the cavity from whence the tumor had come, they saw to their amazement and surprise that not one drop of blood had been shed at the separation of the cancer. The cavity was sufficiently large to receive a small cup and they noticed that the sides were of a beautiful reddish hue. During the next two days, and while they were watching closely they saw the cavity fill up with flesh and a skin formed over it, so that at last there was only a slight scar. At two meetings this lady, filled with enthusiasm, held in her hand a glass vessel containing the cancer, and declared how great things God had done unto her.

Smith - "We must not be content with a mere theory of faith. We must have faith within us so that we move from the ordinary into the extraordinary"

#154   At Oakland a fine-looking young man, a slave to alcohol and nicotine, came along with his wife to see if I could heal him. They stated his case, and I said "Yes, I can heal you in Jesus' Name." I told him to put out his tongue, and I cursed the demon power of alcohol and also cast out the demon power of nicotine. The man knew that he was free. He afterwards became an earnest seeker and within 24 hours was baptized with the Holy Ghost. This is clearly confirming by the Scripture in Mark 16:17 In My Name they shall cast out devils."

Smith - To discern spirits we must dwell with Him who is holy, and He will give the revelation and unveil the mask of Satanic power on all lines.

#155 A preacher, suffering many days from the kick of a horse, walking with great pain and in much distress, made a special call at the hotel in which I was staying, and being led by the Spirit, according to God's Word, I laid hands on the bruised ankle. A fire broke out with burning and healing power, and from that moment on he could walk easily and without pain.

Smith - If we can be open to God, we shall see that He has a greater plan for us in the future than we have ever seen in the past.

#156 A boy came to a meeting on crutches, suffering from a broken ankle. Prayer was made and hands were laid upon him, I had him to walk across the platform. He declared that he had no pain, it was all gone, and carried off his crutches under his arm.

Smith - People of faith have a good report. They never murmur.

Report published in Confidence, p. 23 April - June 1921

#157   In one of the meetings a girl came up and said she had not been able to smell for five years, and I said to her, "You will smell to-day," and in the next meeting she came to testify of being healed, and I called her on the platform, and she made a clear statement of receiving instant healing and smelling. Then at the close of that meeting one came up who had not smelt for twelve years and another for twenty years. I said to them, "You will smell to-night." This sounds like presumption, and certainly is extravagance of language, and on the natural lines could not be understood, but God's Word has creative power, and only in faith of the Word being creative power can we ever expect to see His mighty works made manifestIn the name of Jesus I anointed, laid hands, and commanded the bound to be loosed, and instantly these two women were made to smell the oil. The one that had been bound for twenty years was quite an inspiration by her testimony, as she imparted faith to others by saying she had more pleasure in smelling things on the table than in eating. I cannot stop to give you all the cases, but at this place there were many wonderful deliverances.

Smith - Do not be afraid of persecution. I am never at my best until I am in a conflict, and until I have a fight with the enemy!

#158   A young woman, through many operations, had parts of her hearing senses removed from the head, and asked if that would make any difference to her being made to hear, and knowing that her faith in the Word of God could recreate the defective parts, I at once ministered according to God's Word, believing that instant power would be given. To show that there is a necessity of the one who receives to believe as well as the one who ministers to bring about God's divine plan, she left the platform as she came on apparently no different, but being in the midst of people who were constantly being definitely healed, she appeared again the second time on the platform. She said this time "I am going to believe I shall be healed," and I said, "You, will be healed before you leave the platform," and that night a miracle was performed. From that day she also was a great inspiration to those gathered.

Smith – Let God have His way, whatever the cost.

#159   A young man came to me to be delivered from nicotine poisoning through cigarettes which was wrecking his nerves, and he had tried all means to be free. By faith I cast out this evil power in the Name of Jesus. Oh, if we knew the power of the Name, what it means, and how God intends to honor the simple faith in the Name of JESUS. I had one great desire to present Jesus before the people as the great purpose in the heart of God for the relief of all mankind for spirit, soul and body. After ministering he went away. Three days after, I asked if that young man was in the meeting and there was no response - silence over the place. Then a young woman rose and said that this young man was her husband, and that the desire had all gone for cigarettes or tobacco. Glory to God

Smith – The Holy Ghost is breath. He is Person. It is a marvelous thing to know that He can be in every part of your body!

Report published in Pentecostal Evangel, p. 15 April 17, 1920

#160   On one occasion a woman with a cancer on her nose and upper part of her face came forward to be prayed for and he got her to stand right in front of the people and said to them, "Look at her. She will be here tomorrow night and you will see what God has done for her." He prayed and she left the meeting. The next night she attended the meeting and it was seen that the cancer had gone and there was a new skin on her face. There was another case of a young woman whose face was in a terrible condition through some disease she had contracted. She was prayed for and the next day appeared with a perfectly clean face and the new skin had a brilliant appearance.

Smith - There is power in God's word to make that which does not appear to appear!

#161   A young man came to the meetings to ridicule, but he appeared to be struck dumb, for he could not speak. The brother commanded the demon to come out of him and his tongue was loosed. At another meeting three insane people were sent and put in the front row with a view to creating a tumult, but the brother had discernment, and in the name of Jesus commanded the demons to keep quiet and there was no further trouble. Souls were saved and bodies healed at every meeting and in many instances baptized in the Holy Ghost, with a bursting out in other tongues.

Smith - Always remember, the most difficult things that come to us are to our advantage from God's

Report published in Confidence, p. 23 April - June 1921

#162   At Copenhagen, Denmark: So far, no buildings have been large enough, and hundreds have been turned away." After ministering in a hall which holds 3,000, a hall holding 5,000 was to be obtained. Police on horseback had to control the crowds. "Only by a great squeezing could I get into the hall, assisted by the police officers." Piles of crutches were left behind, the blind saw, epileptic fits dealt with, etc…: "I am at the feet of Jesus, and weep through my address, and God breaks forth upon the people, and there are rows of people each night seeking salvation."

Smith - We have a wonderful God, a God whose ways are past finding out, and whose grace and power are limitless

#163   Bro. Wigglesworth writes: "A poor lame man in a hospital asked the doctor if he could leave to attend the meetings, but was refused permission. He was told that if he broke the regulations he would not be permitted to return. He replied that he did not expect that he would have to return, and it was so." When Bro. Wigglesworth laid hands on him (not knowing all this) he was healed instantly, and left his crutches with the others.

Smith - One man in a meeting, filled with unbelief, can make a place for the devil to have a seat.

#164   I came to seek help myself, being worn out with long unbroken service in the Lord's work. I had not heard of Mr. Wigglesworth before, but I knew that Pastor Barratt, my spiritual father, was there. The next day there was a meeting for healing. After the preaching service I went forward into the other hall and I was surprised to find in a few minutes a crowd following. The hall was soon full with a queue of hundreds of men and women patiently waiting for a touch of God through His servant, and, glory to God, we were not disappointed. As hands were laid upon me the power of God went through me in a mighty way. I was immediately well.

It was wonderful to notice, as the ministry continued, the effect upon the people as the power of the Lord came over them. Some lifted their hands, crying, "I am healed! I am healed!" Some fell on the platform overpowered by the power of the Spirit, having to be helped down. Others walked away as in a dream; others as drunk with new wine, lost to everything but God; but all had faces as transfigured with the glory of the Lord and magnifying Jesus.

A young blind girl, as she was ministered to, cried out, "Oh, how many windows there are in this hall!" During the three weeks the meetings continued the great chapel was crowded daily, multitudes being healed and many saved. The testimony meetings were wonderful. One said, "I was deaf, they prayed, and Jesus healed me." Another, "I had consumption, and I am free," and so on.

Smith - The baptism in the Holy Ghost is an inner activity with an outward manifestation.

#165   In the smaller hall, set apart for those seeking the Baptism of the Holy Ghost, I shall never forget the sight, how the people with eyes closed and hearts up-lifted to God waited. Did the Holy Spirit fall upon them? Of course He did. Here also many were healed. At another place there was a young man whose body was spoiled because of sin, but the Lord is merciful with sinners. He was anointed, and when hands were laid on, the power of God went mightily over him. He said, "I am healed," but being broken down, he cried as a little child confessing his sin; at the same moment the Lord saved him. Glory to God! He went into the large hall and testified to salvation and healing.

Smith – Never trust human plans. God will work mightily when you persist in believing His plan.

#166   The hall held 1,800 people. At nearly every meeting crowds were unable to enter the building, but they waited on often hours and hours for the chance, if any left the building, to step into the place. Here a man with two crutches, his whole body shaking with palsy, is lifted on to the platform. (Behind him five or six hundred more are waiting for help.) This man is anointed and hands laid upon him in the Name of Jesus. He is still shaking. Then he drops one crutch, and after a short time the other one. His body is still shaking, but he takes the first step out in faith! Will it be? He lifts one foot and then the other, walks round the platform. The onlookers rejoice with him. Now he walks around the auditorium. Hallelujah!

Smith - You are always right when you have the backing of the Scriptures. You are never right if you have not a foundation in the Word of God

#167   During a meeting a woman began to shout and shout. The preacher told her to be quiet, but instead she jumped up on a chair, flourishing her arms about, and crying, "I am healed! I am healed! I had cancer in my mouth, and I was unsaved; but during, the meeting, as I listened to the word of God, the Lord has saved me and healed me of cancer in my mouth." She shouts again, "I am saved! I am saved! I am healed of cancer!" She was quite beside herself. The people laughed and cried together.

Smith - Some people would be giants in faith if only they had a shout!

#168   Here was another woman unable to walk, sitting on a chair as she was ministered to. Her experience was the same as hundreds of the others. She rose up, looking around, wondering if after all it was a dream. Suddenly she laughed and said, "My leg is healed." Afterwards she said, "I am not saved," and streams of tears ran down her face. They prayed for her, and later she left the meeting healed and saved and full of joy. We have a wonderful Savior; glory to His Holy Name!

Smith - In me is working a power stronger than every other power. The life that is in me is a thousand times bigger than I am outside.

#169   A man and his son came in a taxi to a meeting. Both had crutches. The father had been in bed two years and was unable to put his leg to the ground. He was ministered to. He dropped both crutches, walking and praising God. When the son saw this he cried out. "Help me too," and after a little while father and son, without crutches and without taxi, walked away from the hall together. That word again is manifested; the same Jesus, the wonder-working Jesus is just the same today.

Smith - God wants us so badly that He has made the condition as simple as He possibly could—only believe.

#170   During three weeks thousands daily attended the meetings. Each morning two or three hundred were ministered to for healing. Each evening the platform was surrounded. Again and again, as each throng retired another company came forward seeking salvation. Here many were baptized in the Holy Ghost. The testimony meetings were wonderful.

Now I will close with a vision a brother had who attended these meetings. He was lost in intercession for the hundreds of sick waiting to be ministered to for healing. He saw an opening from the platform, where the sick were, right into the glory. He saw wonderful beings in the form of men resting who, with interest, looked on. Again he looked at the platform and saw a heavenly Being clothed in white, who all the time was more active than any other in helping the sick, and when He touched them the effect was wonderful. Bent forms were made straight, their eyes shone, they began to glorify and praise the Lord. A Voice said: "Healings are the smallest of all gifts; it is but a drop in the bucket in view of what God has in store for His children. Ye shall do greater works than these."

Smith - God has unlimited resources. Do not doubt it. Hear with the ear of faith.

Report published in Pentecostal Evangel, p. 3 July 23, 1921

#171   There were many remarkable healings. Many suffering with cancer, tumors, tuberculosis, rupture, rheumatism and many other diseases have been miraculously healed through the prayer of faith. We read of one man who was suffering with tuberculosis of the stomach who attended one of our brother's meetings in Switzerland. He was brought in a dying condition on a stretcher in a wagon. By his side was a basket of food, and a friend, knowing his condition, asked the reason for its presence. "I shall eat it going back," was his simple answer, and he did!

Smith - We can never fully understand the wonders of this redemption until we are full of the Holy Ghost

TEACHING FROM SMITH WIGGLESWORTH

* GOD WILL NOT HAVE YOU DRAW PEOPLE AFTER YOURSELF!

Every time you draw anyone to yourself it has a touch of earth. It does not speak of the highest realm of thought of God. There is something about it which cannot bear the light of the Word of God. Keep men's eyes off you, but get their eyes on the Lord. Live in the world without a touch or taint of any natural thing moving you. Live high in the order and authority of God, and see that everything is bearing you on to greater heights and depths and greater knowledge of the love of God.

You will help any assembly you go to, and everybody will get a blessing and will see how much richer they are because you brought them Jesus. Only Jesus! And He is too big for any assembly, and He is little enough to fill every heart. We will always go on to learn of Him. Whatever we know, the knowledge is so small to what He has to give us. And so God's plan for us in giving us Jesus, is all things, for all things consist in Him.

* Seventh-day Adventist will never come into the POWER of CHRIST!

"We are not sufficient to think anything as of ourselves, but our sufficiency is of God." If you go back, you miss the plan. We leave the old order of things. We can never have confidence in the flesh; we cannot touch that. We are in a new order, a spiritual order. It is a new life of absolute faith in the sufficiency of our God in everything that pertains to life and godliness.

You could never come into this place and be a Seventh-day Adventist. The law has no place in you. You are set free from everything. At the same time, like Paul, you are "bound in the Spirit" so that you would not do anything to grieve the Lord.

EXPERIENCES FROM THE AUTHOR

I was Completely Engulfed in Fire, but The Fire Could Not Burn Me!

(2011)

Back in 1981 I began to memorize and meditate on Scriptures declaring that fire cannot consume me.*[Isaiah 43:2 KJV When thou passest through the waters, I will be with thee; and through the rivers, they shall not overflow thee: when thou walkest through the fire, thou shalt not be burned ; neither shall the flame kindle upon thee.]*

I meditated upon the scriptures because I kept burning myself with our woodstove. Through the years, I have maintained these scriptures in my heart. In the summer of 2011, I had an amazing experience when God used these scriptures to come to my rescue, otherwise I would've been burned to death. This particular morning I woke up the actually lost in the Holy Ghost. I mean my mind and my heart was so caught up in God, I was almost drunk in the spirit. I was so heavenly minded at the time that you could even say I was not really much earthly good. In this condition I decided it was a good day to burn the large pile of brush that we had on our property.

This very large brush pile that needed to be burned. It was a very, very hot day. I'm sure it was over 90° outside! I took a 2 ½ gallon plastic gas container to this pile of brush with the full intention of lighting the brush on fire. When I took the cap off of this container, the container was so hot you could see the visible fumes of the gasoline in the air. I had with me one of those long stemmed lighters that you can pick up at any hardware store. I stepped into this pile of very dry brush which was higher than my head by four or five feet.

Then I took this gas container and began to spread gasoline over the pile by splashing it out of the container all over the brush and wood pile. The liquid gasoline was up to the edge of my feet. At the time I wasn't really thinking about what I was doing, I was actually meditating on the word. My son Daniel saw me put the gas container in my left hand. The fumes were visible as they were radiating out of the container. I took the lighter in my right hand and reached down to light the gas. My son Daniel saw what I was about to do and yelled at the top of his lungs Don't, but I only heard him partly because I was so lost in the spirit. I pulled the trigger of the long stemmed lighter and instantly there was an explosion of fire and I was totally engulfed in the flames. I was completely surrounded with fire. My son Daniel said that he could not see me because the fire had swallowed me up.

I remember being in the flames of this fire and it seemed as if there was this invisible force field around me, and that the heat and the flames could not penetrate this invisible force field. I remember standing surrounded completely by fire thinking this is kind of neat. And immediately at the same time something clicked in my head that said: you need to get out of this fire!

Immediately, I began to backtrack away from the fire. When I got out of the fire, I looked down at my body and my clothes and not a flame had kindled upon me. The gas container in my left hand alone should've exploded because of the fumes that were coming out of it.

Once again God had miraculously delivered me from my stupidity. My son Daniel can attest to this story for he saw the whole thing. We rejoiced in God for His great mercy! Of course, my son Daniel was extremely upset with me and was in a state of shock and amazement because he saw me engulfed in the fire. He thought surely I was a dead man!

CHAPTER TEN

Confidence,

#172   Our dear Brother Wigglesworth arrived in Melbourne last Thursday, February 16th, Amongst those who came forward for prayer were several who declared that they had received remarkable and instantaneous healings. A few of those were as follows: One little girl, six years of age, was seen, after prayer by the evangelist, walking out of the front door of the building with her mother, who was delightedly exclaiming to all and sundry, "Look at her! She has never walked in her life before!" A man who had not walked for over four years owing to rheumatoid arthritis, was instantly healed, and after triumphantly passing his stick and crutch up to the platform, gave an impromptu exhibition of the power that had come into his legs by jumping and leaping and praising God.

Others suffering from weak spine, nerve and heart trouble, weak eyesight, asthma, kidney trouble, loss of voice, etc., claimed to have been wonderfully helped.

Since the first night there have been many other wonderful healings. Last night a dear woman who had been unable to walk for 61 years was brought to be prayed for, and—glory be to God!—she got out of her chair and walked, and her husband pushed her chair along, with her walking behind. Praise our covenant-keeping God! Truly He is able to do exceeding abundantly above all that we can ask or think.

There have also been many conversions—at one meeting alone 40 dear ones accepted Jesus as their Lord and Savior—and we are believing for still greater things. The revival showers are falling and God is working. Bless His holy Name!

Just this morning a mother brought her little girl along, who had fallen on a pair of scissors, and cut her mouth so that she could not close it. After the evangelist had laid his hands upon it and prayed, she was able to close her mouth and was quite well. Glory to God!

Smith - Hard things are always opportunities to gain more glory for the Lord. Every trial is a blessing.

Published in Melbourne Argos

#173   At a series of meetings conducted during the last ten days by Mr. Smith Wigglesworth, a Yorkshire evangelist, there have been many "manifestations of healing." Mr. Wigglesworth held his earlier meetings in the Good News Hall, North Melbourne, and at first the attendance was only moderate; but this week it was necessary to transfer to Olympia, as so many persons had to be turned away from the smaller hall.

Last night a large number of persons came "for aid," to use the evangelist's expression; and though he was not successful in all cases, there; were many in which there appeared to be startling and immediate improvement after he had laid his; hands on the afflicted and prayed over them. In one instance a woman who was said to have been very deaf was able to answer him when he spoke to her in an ordinary tone. In another an elderly man, who declared that he had suffered from; noises in the head for ten years, said that he was free from them at last. An elderly woman who was described as almost crippled with rheumatism, was directed to stoop down and touch the ground with her hands. "I don't suppose you have bent your back for some time," Mr. Wigglesworth said. The patient stooped down without effort! Apparently, and was so delighted that she laughed heartily. "No pain and no stiffness now?" asked the evangelist, and she replied that she had none. A girl who had an affliction of the hip and knee, which it was said had prevented her walking without a stick for some years, walked up and down to front of the audience at a rapid pace, whereas she had only been able before to limp slowly with the aid of her stick. "Throw your stick away; burn it," said Mr. Wigglesworth. "You will not want it again." Many other cases gave interesting results.

Smith - They think I am rather unmerciful in my dealing with the sick. No, I have no mercy for the devil.

Published in Melbourne Argos

#174   Further demonstrations of "healing by touch" were given by Mr. Smith Wigglesworth, a Yorkshire evangelist, before a very large assemblage at the Olympia last night. After the evangelist had given an address on the subject of "Faith," he called upon those who had come "for aid" on Tuesday night to testify as to the results; and several persons who had been suffering front deafness, rheumatics, and lameness declared that their ailments had completely gone. Mr. Wigglesworth healing by touch." An elderly man, who said that he had been deaf for years, cried "Hallelujah! Hallelujah!" when asked by Mr. Wigglesworth if he could hear, after hands had been placed on him and he had been prayed over. A woman who, who had stiff legs for over 20 years, and who limped to Olympia on the arm of a relative, ran about the hall in joy after she had been "touched." Another woman, who was said to have been an invalid in a chair for 23 years, declared that her limbs were "beginning to move." She was advised by the evangelist to retain her faith in Jesus Christ and her cure; would be complete. A young woman with pains of long standing "in her back was able to stoop and touch the ground with her hands, and she laughed heartily as she told the audience that her trouble had gone. A woman, who asserted that she had been unable to walk owing to pain in her feet, ran up and down in front of the audience, crying, "Praise the name of the Lord." She declared that her pain vanished when the evangelist touched her.

Smith – In Christ, we are no longer under condemnation. Now, the Heavens are open to us!

Published in Triumphs of Faith

#175   On February 16, 1922, God began His mighty work in Melbourne under the ministry of Mr. Smith Wigglesworth. Testimonies are called for in order that the faith of those who come to receive the Savior's touch may be quickened. A young woman who had been suffering with consumption declared, "I was brought to last Sunday's meeting a poor dying woman, with a disease that was eating into every part of my being. I was full of disease outside as well as in, but Jesus Christ came and loosed me and set me free. I have slept better and eaten more heartily than I have for eight years."

The President of the Methodist Local Preachers' Association testified to having been delivered from nervous trouble. A prominent businessman said, "The first night of this campaign God delivered me from an affliction of the feet I had had for fifty years, since I was two years of age. I am now fifty-two. Ever since I was prayed for I have had no pain. Friends have never seen me do this (stamping his feet). I have no further use for my stick."

A lady testified, - "As soon as I was anointed, the power of God went through me. Also my families have all been saved during these meetings." Mrs. S. said, "While sitting in my seat listening to the Word, God healed me of liver trouble, gallstone, and sciatica. He has also touched my daughter and manifested His power in her body. She was suffering with her feet and had been operated on twice, but as she sat in her seat the Lord began to operate and all pain was gone."

Mrs. B. said, "I was deaf, and suffering with anemia and with my feet, but as soon as hands were laid upon me for healing my ears were opened and I thank God for healing me and for this wonderful salvation for spirit, soul and body which I never saw before."

Mr. L., a Church of England reader, testified that he had been immediately healed of a stiff knee.

Mr. B. testified that a lady of Box Hill, who had been twenty-two years in an invalid's chair, rose and walked after Mr. Wigglesworth had ministered to her in the Name of Jesus.

Mr. V., a suburban Protestant Federation Society Secretary, testified that a friend was healed the night before of rhomboid arthritis of four years' standing, and had discarded stick and crutch. The friend rose in the audience saying, "I am the one."

Mr. J., of Spring Vale, who had been deaf for twenty years, was healed, and also his wife, who had sat in a wheel chair for six years; both were immediately healed. The empty chair was wheeled to the railway station, while the woman testified to all bystanders of the great things the Lord had done for her. Many were healed through the application of anointed handkerchiefs.

Smith - God works mightily when you persist in believing Him.

Report published in Confidence,

#176   I feel I must express my deep gratitude for blessing received. Only those who have been in the furnace of affliction can realize the joy of deliverance. It seems too wonderful. After fourteen years of anguish, sleeplessness, and spiritual depression, caused by the bondage of the adversary, these are things of the past. As Bro. Wigglesworth says, consumption is of the devil, and only the Lion of Judah could have delivered me from this dread scourge, which had made my body a mass of corruption. Hallelujah!   KATHLEEN GAY.

Smith - Hear with the ear of faith! *See with the eye of Faith*

#177   I was prayed for in Melbourne, and the evil spirit was commanded to come out. I had a polypus growth in my nose. It had been there eighteen years. When I came home from Melbourne the growth broke up and came away, for which I praise God. I had also it pain under my left breast which had troubled me twelve years. I think it was leakage of the heart, as sorrow had caused it in the first place. At times I used to vomit blood. I have deliverance from that also. All praise to our wonder-working Jesus!   MRS. T. SIMCOCK.

Smith - When the devil is manifesting himself, then is the time to deal with him!

#178   I have had liver problems all my life. When as a girl I was treated by the best doctors, but it always returned, and at times I was unable to turn in bed without help. The last twelve months my kidneys were bad, and my legs swollen much with cramp. I had also varicose veins, with lumps larger than an egg. Now, glory to God, all has gone—disappeared—as soon as hands were laid upon me in the name of Jesus.

Smith - God is everything the Word says He is. We need to get acquainted with Him through the Word.

#179   L. M Buchanan writes of the meetings held in Sydney: "A woman who was to have undergone an operation yesterday went to the doctor, who said that there was neither misplacement nor inflammation". When she told him the reason he said that she would soon be worse. Another who was to have undergone several operations because the work could not be done in one, testifies that she was free, and that the Lord had lengthened her leg two inches and that instead of limping she is now walking perfectly. Another mother brought her little boy who had fits all day long. He was prayed for at the meeting and after the evangelist had gone he had a fit worse than before. The unbelievers' sarcasm was to be heard all over the building. Two days later the mother returned to say that the child had not had another fit. A little girl aged five years old, who had been stone-deaf three years, received her healing at once. The healings have been too numerous to mention and the preaching of the Word was wonderful."

At the meeting at Geelong, one testified. "I had a withered hand for 14 years. When Mr. Wigglesworth was here a month ago it was cured."

Smith - I believe God wants to bring us all to a definite place of unswerving faith and confidence in Himself.

#180   At Parkes a quarter of the population tried to get into the theatre. The preaching was wonderful and also the healings. A little girl, deaf for six years, eardrums burst and bleeding, was instantly healed. Her brother, blind in one eye, received his sight immediately when he was prayed for. The daily papers say that no meetings on a religious line equal to these had ever been experienced in Parkes.

Smith - God has something better for you than you have ever had in the past. Come NOW into His fulness, power, life and victory!

#181   A teacher at Bunibank Methodist Sunday school testifies to healing of rheumatoid arthritis. "A doctor examined me in the beginning of December, 1911, and told me I would need new joints to walk. He said he would defy anyone to cure me, and although I improved in health I did not walk better. On April 4th I went to be prayed with, and believed God would heal me. As hands were placed on my head in the name of Jesus, I felt the power of God go right through me. After the meeting I walked down three flights of stairs without a stick for the first time for sixteen years, and I have no use for a stick since. I have always tried to impress upon the juniors the power of prayer, but I had not realized I would have to demonstrate it in my own life. After testifying in the Sunday school, I asked all who were Christians or who would became so to stand. Every teacher and every scholar stood, and so we sang the Doxology. Men of the world have told me 'It has set them thinking.' There is no evidence now that I had ever rheumatoid arthritis. Praise God!"

Smith - The man of God does not experiment. He is not moved by outward observation but by divine revelation.

#182   A dairyman had for 3 years suffered with chronic gastritis and paralysis of both legs from the hips downward and could only drag along with crutches. He testifies, "On June 4th I attended the Town Hall. I was anointed, hands were laid on me, and Mr. Wigglesworth told me to walk. I handed him my crutches and walked home."

Smith - In every weakness, God will be your strength.

#183   For 14 years I have had a cyst on the back of my neck. It increased in size to the size of an egg. The next morning I found it had completely disappeared."

Smith - "By the grace of God, I want to impart the Word and bring you to a place where you will dare to act on it!"

#184   A lady testifies, "Over 3 years ago varicose veins in my legs broke. I was twice in hospital, but when I used the legs the veins burst open. The last time they were cut and an ulcer formed. I had to walk with a stick, and could only limp. I went to the Town Hall. I had faith that Jesus would heal me. The pain ceased and I was able to leave my stick and walk to the car. My leg is sound and the ulcer is daily healing. I am now able to wash and do my housework."

Smith - "When we don't allow ourselves to be taken away from the Word of God, then comes the inspiration, the life, the activity, the glory!"

#185   Another Wellington lady says that her son (age 11) 6 years ago broke his arm. It was badly set and he could not bend it properly. It was massaged for 12 months without any benefit. It is healed. Also her daughter, who suffered from adenoids, was healed.

Smith - "God wants you pure in heart. He wants you to have an intense desire after holiness."

#186   A lady from Ngaio, aged 20, has suffered from double curvature of the spine from infancy. She could not walk until 4 years of age and could only rise from the floor by pulling herself up with both hands. One leg was 3 inches shorter and less in circumference. She went to many hospitals and was sent home incurable. She states, "As soon as hands were laid upon me I was healed, my spine was straightened, in a few days my leg lengthened, and my hip, which was diseased, was healed."

Smith - "The devil is a liar."

Report published in Pentecostal Evangel

#187 For many years I suffered from bronchitis and asthma. I had pains in my chest and was very short of breath. I went to the meetings at the Olympia and Mr. Wigglesworth laid hands on me, and rebuked the evil spirit. I felt the power of God go right through me. I was immediately healed, and have not had a pain since.

Smith - "When you receive the Holy Ghost, you receive God's Gift, in whom are all the gifts of the Spirit."

#188 I was on Feb. 4th. 1922, dressing my little girls when Thelma, aged 4, fell. I picked her up and found her bleeding at the mouth. The scissors were in her hand, and she ran the point through her lips. Her mouth began to swell, and I said. "Dear Jesus, don't let her go any further." I hurried to the Good News Hall and the secretary carried her to Mr. Wigglesworth, who was at breakfast. In a few minutes the lady brought her back, with her mouth closed, and perfectly healed. The child told me that the gentleman had laid his hands on her lips and prayed, and that Jesus had made her better. J. M. Henderson.

Smith – "There is power in the name of Jesus."

#189 I was born with a weak, crooked ankle. I was anointed at the Olympia and it was immediately straightened and made strong. I had to wear a specially formed boot and straps, these are no use to me now. I have bought ordinary boots. Medical men have attended me and could do nothing. Lily Ward.

Smith - "I am never happier in the Lord than when I am in a bedroom with a sick person."

#190   Brother Smith Wigglesworth of England has arrived in this country after a mighty ministry A New Zealand newspaper, reporting our brother's meetings says, "Last night two hundred presented themselves for healing. Many were able to throw away crutches and sticks immediately. Others with goiter, rheumatism, partial blindness and deafness. A woman crippled with rheumatism, walks quickly across the floor; stutterers read the Lord's prayer without stuttering. An old woman, deaf and dumb, says 'Jesus.' A man whose leg had been broken with a bad mend walks away smiling and confident without his crutches."

Smith - "When we come to the place of impossibilities, it is the grandest place for us to see the possibilities of God."

Report published in Pentecostal Evangel

#191   Wiggelsworth not only preaches the Word of God but acts it out literally; puts it into practice. To quote him, "God demands of every believer who has been baptized in the Holy Spirit that he should have some 'acts'. If you do not have them, you had better get face to face with God and demand from Him your acts."

When time was given for testimony in one of the services, people arose all over the house and testified to having been healed of many diseases: A woman healed of heart trouble, another of high blood pressure; a man of heart trouble, another of gangrene; other healings of broken arches, a sore limb of which a women had been afflicted for three years, indigestion of long standing, itching boils, lumbago, rheumatism after being afflicted thirty-eight years, insomnia, etc., etc.

Smith – When you take up God's Word, you get the truth. Remember, God is not a man that He should lie.

#192   "It will rejoice your heart to hear the beautiful testimonies which are still coming in from those who were helped and blest in your meetings here in Australia. The dear people do not forget those beautiful spiritual feasts they had every morning. Do you remember that dear woman in J,---- who was too ill to be brought in the church? She was put in the vestry, had to be carried in, was wrapped up in bandages. Well, she is now a living miracle, is going around doing her own work as well as anyone. It was a Baptist minister who brought this woman and he is now seeking to be filled with the Holy Ghost.

Smith – "Forgive, and the Lord will forgive you."

#193   "Brother F. was telling us of a dear ten year old boy who did not develop; he was born deficient. As you prayed with him, he felt something go out of him and he is now perfectly delivered, and is as intelligent as any boy. Another lady was suffering with chronic asthma and was so ill, especially at night. You prayed for her and she is now perfectly healed. These are lasting cases for which we give God the glory.

Smith – "Always remember, the most difficult things that come to us are to our advantage from God's side."

#194 "Not many weeks ago a lady who is a professor of music, in one of your meetings was suffering with a severe pain at the back of her neck and in her nerves. As she sat in her seat and heard you give forth the precious Word of God, she called on the Name of the Lord and was perfectly healed. She has not had any return of the trouble. An old lady who was wonderfully healed by the Lord is going around as happy as can be. She could scarcely walk about the streets, now is as nimble as a child. It is beautiful to see her. You will probably remember the family in which you were used of the Lord in bringing husband and wife together. God continues to bless that family, and now four of them have received the baptism of the Holy Spirit according to Acts 2:4."

Smith - The greatest weakness of a preacher is when he draws men to himself.

Report published in Pentecostal Evangel

#195 The campaign began March 5th in a hall capable of holding a thousand people. From the first night it was a great success, hundreds being saved.

Not a night passed without many standing up and reaching out their hands to heaven, calling out, "Jesus save me! Jesus deliver me!" Each night the evangelist would single out people in the audience who were in pain, and would pray for them. Immediately after prayer was offered the suffering ones would testify that they were free, from pain. If it was a case of stiff limbs, they were made to exercise them by walking up and down, running, stamping their feet, or waving their arms about in order to test whether the pain had actually gone.

Smith - The Word of God is supernatural in origin, eternal in duration, infinite in scope, regenerative in power & infallible in authority.

#196 One night a woman came up the aisle, walking in pain, her body all doubled up, and she finally fell on the floor in front of the platform, the pain was so great that Brother Wigglesworth jumped off the platform and put his hands upon her, and said, "In the name of Jesus I bind this pain and loose this woman." Immediately she ran up and down the aisle, free from pain, and then went and sat down to listen to the message. She was perfectly whole. This demonstration had a great effect upon the crowd.

Smith - Begin your day in the Spirit and you will be conscious of the guidance of the Spirit right through the day.

#197 Some nights the evangelist prayed for over five hundred people, many of them coming hundreds of miles bringing their sick with them - the blind, deaf, dumb, lame, palsied, consumptive, eaten up with cancer, tumor's, epilepsy, weak-minded, deranged, crippled. God worked mighty miracles; blind eyes were opened, deaf ears unstopped, stammering tongues spoke, men on crutches put them over their shoulder and went away, stiff joints were made supple, headaches and fevers vanished, asthma was treated as an evil power and cast it out in the name of Jesus.

Smith – "This blessed Book brings such life and health and peace, and such an abundance that we should never be poor anymore."

#198   Handkerchiefs were brought in an ever-increasing number and piled high upon the platform. So many were brought (quite 500 some nights) that a fairly large suitcase was necessary to hold them all. One night, while our attention was diverted, a boy stole six new handkerchiefs that had been brought. Two nights later he came back with them confessing that he had not been able to sleep since he had taken them. Many wonderful cures were wrought through this means. One was taken to a sanatorium and placed on a consumptive boy. The boy is wonderfully better, is putting on flesh and looking healthy.

Smith - It is my business to make people either glad or mad. I have a message from heaven that will not leave people as I find them

#199   Many people were helped by rising from their seats in faith and saying, "Jesus heal me," without the prayers of the evangelist at all. One woman, who had eruptions on her arms and burning sensations caused by these eruptions, was healed as she sat in her seat. Truly these were wonderful days. God's Spirit was poured out and Jesus was glorified.

Smith - Remember, the most trying time is the most helpful time. In your weakness, God will make you strong.

Report published in Redemption Tidings

#200 The follow-on meetings have been wonderfully blessed. One woman in the Sunday morning meeting, after Brother Wigglesworth had left, was healed of three diseases. She came on the following Wednesday bringing fifteen friends with her, eleven of whom were saved that night as we gave the altar call. I had the job of immersing eight in water while Brother Wigglesworth was here. The youngest being a Singhalese girl, seven years old. She had a wonderful testimony, and on the morning of her baptism, she had a vision of Jesus. It was a joy to my soul to take her in my arms and bury her with Christ in the water.

Smith - Thousands have missed wonderful blessings because they have not had faith to move.

Report published in Pentecostal Evangel,

#201 As a testimony of the efficiency of prayer in healing sicknesses, Mrs. Spelder of Kandy, who suffered from a virulent cancer in the stomach and whose case was abandoned as hopeless by scientific medical men, on Tuesday confessed to having been completely freed of the disease by Mr. Wigglesworth's prayer. People of all sorts, of all ages and classes, of diverse religions and professions, have attended Mr. Wigglesworth's meetings, and though there have been scoffers among them nearly all of them have gone away impressed by his words and his actions.

Smith - Oh for a simple faith to receive all that God so lavishly offers!

#202　Mr. Wigglesworth prays, the ailments ranging from headaches and pains in the body to rheumatism, catarrh, blindness, deafness, etc. Not a few children are brought by doting mothers and women of advanced age by loving relatives, and if their derangements are not set a right on the first day they come again and yet again. Confirmed drunkards and smokers have been purged of the desire for intoxicants, and persons suffering from consumption and diseases due to dissolute lives have admitted to have been cured by Mr. Wigglesworth's prayer and their own. Many prominent people have been attracted to the hall, from which none could go away without a profound impression of Mr. Wigglesworth – his deep voice, his simple but weighty words, his remarkable personality, and above all the perfect confidence of his actions, as when he says "In the name of Jesus, come out of this woman," addressing the evil spirit possessing the patient before him. "Are you healed?" he asks, and if the reply is in the affirmative, "Praise the Lord" he adds.

Smith - Lord, give us, thy servants, great searching's of heart, great decisions of will, and great assurances through the blood of Jesus.

#203　A lady resident in Kandy was brought down to Colombo about two weeks ago. She was suffering from cancer and was in "extremis," and the doctors in Kandy had given up all hopes. Eminent physicians consulted in Colombo were also of the same opinion. The day Evangelist Wigglesworth arrived the relatives of the lady called on him, at the Glad Tidings Hall at Borella, and asked him to see the patient. As he was unable to go on that same day he gave them a piece of cloth, which he blessed, to be placed on the seat of the trouble pending his arrival on the next day. Immediately the cloth was placed on the patient, she said she felt relief and that the agony she was suffering for weeks and the spasms of pain left her. The Evangelist saw her the next day and cast out what he termed the "evil spirit that was afflicting her in the form of a cancer," and the lady is today perfectly well and able to get about. She is to testify at tonight's meeting conducted by Smith Wigglesworth.

Smith - Prayer is without accomplishment unless it is accompanied by faith.

Report published in Redemption Tidings

#204   The campaign began in a large hall capable of holding a thousand people. From the first night it was a great success, hundreds were saved, not a night passing by without many standing up in response to the appeals of the Evangelist stretching their hands up to heaven, calling out, "Jesus save me, Jesus deliver me," and then, as they stood up, the Evangelist would pray, asking the Lord to have mercy upon them and save them; then the whole audience would sing, "I do believe, I will believe, that Jesus died for me, that on the Cross, He shed His blood, for sin to set me free." Every night he would single out people in the audience, who were in pain and pray for them, and immediately after prayer was offered the suffering one would testify that they were free from pain. If it was a case of stiff limbs, they were made to exercise them by walking up and down, running, stamping their feet, or waving their arms about in order to test whether the pain had actually gone or not.

Smith - "I believe God will always turn out to meet you...if you dare to believe him"

#205   One night a woman came up the aisle walking in pain, her body all doubled up, and she finally fell on the floor in front of the platform, the pain was so great. Mr. Wigglesworth jumped off the platform and put his hands upon her and said, in the Name of Jesus Christ, I bind this pain and loose this woman, and she immediately ran up and down the aisle free from pain, and then went and sat down to listen to the message perfectly whole. This demonstration had a great effect upon the crowd.

Smith - "It is impossible to overestimate the importance of being filled with the Spirit."

#206   Some nights the Evangelist had to pray for over five hundred people. Many of them coming hundreds of miles, bringing their sick with them – the blind, deaf, dumb, lame, paralyzed, consumptive, eaten up with cancer, tumor's, epilepsy, weak-minded, deranged, crippled, with rheumatism and many other kinds of diseases. They came an increasing multitude, and God worked mighty miracles. Blind eyes being opened, deaf ears were unstopped, stammering tongues spoke plain, men on crutches put them over their shoulders and went away, stiff joints were made supple, headaches and fevers vanished, asthma was cursed as an evil power and cast out in the Name of Jesus. It was a wonderful sight to see them coming, and to know that those who had faith, went away rejoicing, in a Living, Loving, Tender-hearted Savior, who had delivered them from the power of the devil that had bound them for weeks and months, and years, or a lifetime.

We know that many wonderful cures have been wrought in this way, eruptions have vanished, and a case of insanity was wonderfully helped. The father brought a handkerchief for his son in the asylum; after it had been prayed over it was taken to the asylum, placed on the son's head, and he at once began to speak like a normal being. Another one was taken to a sanatorium, and placed on a consumptive boy; the message brought from the sanatorium says the boy is wonderfully better, putting on flesh and looking healthy. Drunkard's lives have been changed by these means, desires for gambling have gone, and many wonderful deliverances have taken place. Glory to Jesus.

Smith - "Before God could bring me to this place He has broken me a thousand times."

TEACHING FROM SMITH WIGGLESWORTH

*God Is Looking for Those Who Are Desperate For HIM!

God is looking, God is wanting men and women who are willing to submit, and SUBMIT, and SUBMIT, and yield, and YIELD, and YIELD to the Holy Spirit until their bodies are saturated and soaked through and through with God, until you realize that God your Father has you in such condition that at any moment He can reveal His will to you and communicate whatever He wants to say to you.

God wants us to be in a place where the least breath of heaven makes us all on fire, ready for everything. You say, "How can I have that?" Oh, you can have that as easy as anything. "Can I?" Yes, it is as simple as possible. "How?" Let heaven come in; let the Holy Ghost take possession of you, and when He comes into your body you will find out that that is the keynote of the spirit of joy and the spirit of rapture, and if you will allow the Holy Ghost to have full control you will find you are living in the Spirit, and you will find out that the opportunities will be God's opportunities, and there is a difference between God's opportunities and ours. You will find you have come to the right place at the right time, and you will speak the right word at the right time and in the right place, and you will not go a warfare at your own charge.

* Some times when you pray for the sick you have to get rough.

But you are not dealing with a person, you are dealing with the Satanic forces that are binding the person. Your heart is full of love and compassion to all, but you are moved to a holy anger as you see the place the devil has taken in the body of the sick one, and you deal with his position with a real forcefulness. One day a pet dog followed a lady out of her house and ran all around her feet. She said to the dog, "My dear, I cannot have you with me today." The dog wagged its tail and made a big fuss. She said, "Go home, my dear." But the dog did not go. At last she shouted roughly, "Go home," and off it went. Some people deal with the devil like that. The devil can stand all the comfort you like to give him. Cast him out! You are dealing not with the person, you are dealing with the devil. Demon power must be dislodged in the name of the Lord: You are always right when you dare to deal with sickness as with the devil. Much sickness is caused by some misconduct, there is something wrong, there is some neglect somewhere, and Satan has had a chance to get in. It is necessary to repent and confess where you have given place to the devil, and then he can be dealt with.

EXPERIENCES FROM THE AUTHOR

As I Slammed my Broken Foot Down as Hard as I Could, God Instantly Healed It!

One day I had to climb our 250 foot radio tower in order to change the light bulb on the main beacon. However, in order to climb the tower, I had to first find the keys; which I never did. Since I could not find the keys to get the fence open, I did the next best thing—I simply climbed over the fence.

This idea turned out not to be such a wonderful idea after all! With all of my climbing gear hanging from my waist, I climbed the fence to the very top. At this point, my rope gear became entangled in the fencing. As I tried to get free, I lost my balance and fell backwards off the fence. Trying to break my fall, I got my right foot down underneath me. In which case, I came down on my foot, when it was still crooked. I hit the ground with my foot being turned on its side and I felt something break in the ankle. I knew instantly I had a broken foot, ankle.

Most normal people would have climbed back over the fence, go set up a doctor's appointment, have their foot x-rayed, and then placed into a cast. But I am not a normal-thinking person, at least according to the standards of the modern day church. When I broke my foot, I followed my routine of confessing my stupidity to God, and asking Him to forgive me for my stupidity. Moreover, I spoke to my foot and commanded it to be healed in the name of Jesus Christ of Nazareth. When I had finished speaking to my foot, commanding it to be healed, and then praising and thanking God for the healing, there seem to be no change in its condition.

The Scripture that came to my heart was where Jesus declared, "The kingdom of heaven suffereth violence, and the violent take it by force!" Based completely upon this scripture, I decided to climb the tower by faith, with a broken foot. Please do not misunderstand me, my foot hurt so bad I could hardly stand it. And yet, I had declared that I believed I was healed.

There were three men watching me as I took the Word of God by faith. I told them what I was about to do, and they looked at me like as if I had lost my mind. I began to climb the 250 foot tower, one painful step at a time. My foot hurt so bad that I was hyperventilating within just twenty to thirty feet up the tower. It literally felt like I was going to pass out from shock at any moment. Whenever I got to the point of fainting, I would connect my climbing ropes to the tower, stop and take a breather. It seemed to take me forever to get to the top.

Even so, I finally did reach the very top of the tower and replaced the light bulb that had gone out.

Usually I can come down that tower within 10 minutes, because I would press my feet against the tower rods, and then slide down, just using my hands and arms to lower myself at a very fast pace. However, in this situation, my foot could not handle the pressure of being pushed up against the steel. Consequently, I had to work my way down very slowly. After I was down, I slowly climbed over the fence one more time. I hobbled my way over to my vehicle, and drove up to the church office. The men who had been watching this unfold, were right behind me.

I hobbled my way into the front office; which is directly across the street from the radio tower. I informed the personnel that I had broken my foot, showing the my black and blue extreemly swollen foot. It did not help that I had climbed with it! I was them that I was going home to rest. At the same time, however, I told them that I believed I was healed.

Going to my house, which is directly across from the main office of the church parking lot, I made my way slowly up the stairs to our bedroom. I found my wife in the bedroom putting away our clothes. Slowly and painfully I pulled the shoe and sock off of the broken foot. What a mess! It was fat, swollen, black and blue all over. I put a pillow down at the end of the bed, and carefully pulled myself up onto the bed. Lying on my back, I tenderly placed my broken, black and blue foot onto the pillow. No matter how I positioned it, the pain did not cease. I just laid there squirming, moaning and sighing.

As I was lying there trying to overcome the shock that kept hitting my body, I heard the audible voice of God. He said to me: "What are you doing in bed?"

God really got my attention when I heard him with my natural ears. My wife would testify that she heard nothing.

Immediately in my heart I said: Lord I'm just resting.

Then He spoke to my heart with the still quiet voice very clearly, Do you always rest at this time of day?

No, Lord, I replied.(It was about 3 o'clock in the afternoon)

He then spoke to my heart and said this, I thought you said you were healed?

At that very moment the gift of faith exploded inside of me. I said, "Lord, I am healed!"

Immediately, I pushed myself up off of the bed, grabbed my sock and shoe, and struggled to put them back on. And what a tremendous struggle it was! My foot was so swollen that it did not want to go into the shoe. My wife was watching me as I fought to complete this task.

You might wonder what my wife was doing this whole time as I was fighting this battle of faith. She was doing what she always does, just watching me and shaking her head. I finally got the shoe on my swollen, black and blue foot. I put my foot down on the floor and began to put my body weight upon it. When I did, I almost passed out. At that moment, a holy anger exploded on the inside of me. I declared out loud, "I am healed in the name of Jesus Christ of Nazareth!" With that declaration, I took my right (broken) foot, and slammed it down to the floor as hard as I possibly could.

When I did that, I felt the bones of my foot break even more. Like the Fourth of July, an explosion of blue, purple, red, and white exploded in my brain and I passed out. I came to lying on my bed. Afterward, my wife informed me that every time I passed out, it was for about ten to twenty seconds. The moment I came to, I jumped right back up out of bed. The gift of faith was working in me mightily. I got back up and followed the same process again, "In the name of Jesus Christ of Nazareth I am healed," and slammed my foot down once more as hard as I could! For a second time, I could feel the damage in my foot

increasing. My mind was once again wrapped in an explosion of colors and pain as I blacked out.

When I regained consciousness, I immediately got up once again, repeating the same process. After the third time of this happening I came to with my wife leaning over the top of me. I remember my wife saying as she looked at me, "You're making me sick. I can't watch you do this." She promptly walked out of our bedroom, and went downstairs.

The fourth time I got up declaring, "In the name of Jesus Christ of Nazareth I am healed," and slammed my foot even harder! Once more, multiple colors of intense pain hit my brain. I passed out again! I got up the fifth time, angrier than ever. This was not a demonic or proud anger. This was a divine gift of violent I-will-not-take-no-for-an-answer type of faith. I slammed my foot down the fifth time, "In the name of Jesus Christ of Nazareth I am healed!"

The minute my foot slammed into the floor, for the fifth time, the power of God hit my foot. I literally stood there under the quickening power of God, and watched my foot shrink and become normal. All of the pain was completely and totally gone. I pulled back my sock, and watched the black and blue in my foot disappear to normal flesh color. I was healed! Praise God, I was made whole! I went back to the office, giving glory to the Lord and showing the staff my healed foot.

IMPORTANT INFORMATION: YOUR PREPARATION TO RECEIVE HEALING BEFORE YOU ARE PRAYED FOR & HANDS ARE LAID ON YOU! THIS WILL GREATLY INCREASE YOUR OPPORTUNITY TO BE HEALED!

#1 1st realize and boldly confess, God wants to heal me more than I want to be healed. It is God's will to heal me, no matter what I have done. It gives God great pleasure to heal people because he is a God of love and compassion.

#2 Go through the 4 Gospels looking for every time Jesus healed people. Notice the Scriptures declare he healed them all. Every single person Jesus prayed for was healed. Most instantaneous, some progressive as they went, but they were healed.

#3 Recognize that Jesus was the perfect will of the father manifested in the flesh. That everything Jesus did was based upon the fact that the father told him to do it. Hebrews says that Jesus Christ is the same yesterday today and forever. If he ever did it once, he will do it again.

#4 Get It Out Of Your Head, that you do not deserve to be healed. None of us deserve to be healed, it is God's mercy, love and kindness. Get it out of your head that the sickness you have is Paul's thorn in the flesh, or God trying to teach you something.

These are all lies from the devil. Jesus Christ, God the Father, and the Holy Ghost are all eager and desiring to make you whole.

#5 Try to prepare your heart with great faith and expectation for what God is going to do through the whole day if possible. Get ready because God will not only heal that one particular problem you have, but he will be doing many other wonderful things for you in when you prayed for.

#6 Began to boldly declared to yourself(and others if you want to) that when hands are laid on me, Jesus Christ himself will touch my sick disease body and I WILL BE MADE WHOLE! NO IFS, ANDS OR BUTS! I WILL BE MADE WHOLE! TODAY IS MY DAY TO BE HEALED, TO BE DELIVERED, TO BE SET FREE.

#7 BEGIN TO PRAISE GOD RIGHT NOW, THIS VERY MOMENT FOR YOUR HEALING, FOR YOUR DELIVERANCE, FOR YOUR FREEDOM!
I AM EXCITED ABOUT WHAT WE'RE GOING TO SEE GOD DO IN YOU, TO YOU, AND EVEN THROUGH YOU!
Sincerely: Dr Michael H Yeager

ABOUT THE AUTHOR

Dr. Michael and Kathleen Yeager have served as pastors/apostles, missionaries, evangelist, broadcasters and authors for almost four decades. Up to this time they have authored ten books. Their three son, daughter and daughter in law work with them in the ministry. Michael and Kathleen have been married sense 1978. They have helped start over 27 churches. They flow in the gifts of the Holy Spirit, teaching the word of God, with wonderful signs following and confirming God's word. In 1983 they began Jesus is Lord Ministries international. The same year the Lord spoke to Dr. Yeager to go on TV. From then to now they have been actively involved in broadcast media for the propagation of the gospel.
Jesus is Lord Ministries International
3425 Chambersburg Rd.

Biglerville, Pennsylvania 17307

Websites:

www.jilmi.org
www.docyeager.org
www.wordbroadcast.org
www.hellsreal.com

Horrors of Hell, Splendors of Heaven
by Dr. Michael Yeager
$15.00

When you read the true story of Dr. Michael Yeager's encounter with the afterlife, you too will realize the indescribable depth of the horrors of hell, and the unimaginable splendors of heaven. Fall into the gut-wrenching realms of the damned, enter into the divine gates of heaven, and be escorted by an angel into an amazing dimension of beauty and nature. End your journey upon the sea of glass before the thunder and lightning of God's throne. Along the way, you will discover answers to your deepest questions about the afterlife. As you take the journey from hell to heaven and back, the revelations you receive will be eternal.